SUCCESS PATHS BUSINESS SERIES

How to Plan and Budget a Successful Small Business

Ted Clifton

How to Plan and Budget a Successful Small Business
Ted Clifton
Paperback edition 978-1-77342-127-8
Ebook edition 978-1-77342-126-1

Published by PurpleSage Books LLC
www.TedClifton.com

Produced by IndieBookLauncher.com
www.IndieBookLauncher.com
Cover Design: Saul Bottcher
Interior Design and Typesetting: Saul Bottcher

The body text of this book is set in Adobe Caslon.

Contents

Introduction

This book is about thinking. Thinking about a business using numbers. Business owners have many plans for their business, which often are in their head and not spelled out. If that works for you, stick with it—but often the plans are a little mushy and seldom do actual results get compared to those once thought about plans.

I'm a strong advocate for planning with numbers. This isn't perfect, but when you talk about your sales plans and what you think that means to your business—it is important to put those plans into a spreadsheet and test your ideas.

My goal is not to turn every business owner into an accountant—my goal is to give you the tools that can turn your dreams into reality. It's not the only tool but I think planning, budgeting, and doing financial analysis are very important tools and hopefully, I can make that case in this book.

1

Why Plan and Budget?

Planning

Why do businesses plan and budget? Often for small businesses the answer is they don't. That is something big companies do, not my two-man shop, what's the point? I know what is going on because I'm the one doing it. That is a pretty good reason to not do a lot of planning, but even the smallest business should do some. Why?

Planning is a way to identify areas that might be a problem and address those concerns before they become "real" problems. And a budget is just a plan with numbers assigned to it. Many small businesspeople will lay out a written plan for their day or their week, such as a "to do" list. Or a list of jobs that need to be accomplished over some period. That is a plan.

Small business owners usually do not have the experience to develop a detailed financial plan because they are not familiar with all the elements of their business. This, of course, is one of the reasons to do a budget; so, you become familiar with what makes up the numbers you will see on a financial statement. If you are running a small retail business, this is not difficult. If your business is a small manufacturing business—it can become very complicated.

For examples throughout this book, I will use a one location restaurant. A restaurant has many similarities to a retail business, with walk in customers, and shares attributes to a manufacturing operation. While preparing food doesn't sound like a manufacturing business—it is. Making a hamburger is not that much different than manufacturing a car—except, of course, the scale of the product. Each must first be planned for by buying materials that will be assembled or made on site, those parts must be readily available on a strict timeline and the proper number of people available to assemble the parts. And to even add more to the food challenge, it must be done based on input from the customer in real time. "I don't want any pickles, extra cheese, mustard and mayo and no lettuce". Usually not a problem experienced in making a car.

The restaurant gives us something we can understand and offers complicated potential problems in planning. That big problem is not knowing what revenues will be. Back to the car manufacturer, you could plan on building one thousand cars but only get orders for ten. However, your car has value, just not enough value for people to buy it—so you give a 20% discount and now you've sold eight hundred and ten. So, a 50% discount and you've sold them all. Did you make money? Probably not, but you reduced your loss and can reinvest to make a better car next time. The hamburger, a whole different problem. Can't sell old hamburgers, no matter the discount. So, in many ways you must plan better as a restaurant owner than General Motors.

One of the innovations in food service was what was called fast food. Those innovators were not trying to make food fast, they were trying to make food on an assembly line basis and make it cheaper. The problem was obvious. Making food as fast as you and your employees are able creates a lot of product. Without customers, it is just a lot of waste. If you stopped and waited for customers, you were back to a custom-made product with all the inherited inefficiencies and costs. The only way to solve that problem was to offer hamburgers at a ridiculous price. A 10-cent hamburger when the competition might be 30 cents or more. Many of these cheap places made their hamburgers as fast as they could, even without customer orders, and would then wrap them in foil and place them under heat lamps. The product was waiting for the customers and immediately served; "fast food" became a reality.

McDonald's was the Henry Ford approach to making cars turned into a food production line.

Obviously, the customers loved it. The customers were willing to give up a custom-made product for a cheap price and instant delivery. It probably would not have worked if either of those elements had not been in place. Instant delivery at the regular price would not have been enough incentive. The customer knew they were giving up some quality but measured the benefits against the drawbacks and a whole new industry was born.

Was planning involved in this concept—of course it was. I personally don't know if the McDonald brothers developed columnar pads of estimated times and costs per burger or if it was mostly in their heads, but every businessperson plans. Some of those plans work out, some do not. But I would bet you a plug nickel that Dick and Mac McDonald had worked out a lot of the bugs on paper before they started their production line approach to mass produce cheap burgers.

Back to the big problem in planning, not knowing what revenue will be. How do you do that? I would think most new restauranters just guess. Could be they have some experience working at a restaurant and they can use that experience to estimate their revenues. You could start by estimating the maximum people you could serve or seat in a particular location. Breaking that down to how long they would stay and then estimating revenue per customer, and you might reach an upper limit number.

At best for most new businesses, you come up with an average, of course the world does not do average very well. So, you will experience up and down revenue. One of the obvious problems in our example of a restaurant is that you can't staff based on an average. Some days you will be short and some days you would have excess payroll. Very few days are average so most days you miss the mark. Which means you either have unhappy customers or you have too high payroll costs.

Matching your revenue with your costs is at the heart of why you plan. Without some plan and understanding, you will always be guessing. Even with a plan you are guessing, somewhat, but as you guess you get better at it, so your plans become more meaningful. If you're not planning and just reacting, you'll never master the art of planning and will always be missing the goal.

I've worked with many business owners regarding plans, goal setting and Key Performance Indicators, which usually involves some "guessing". They often hate it. They want real numbers. What's the point of planning ahead if you don't know for sure what will happen?

But let's think about that a minute. You're opening a restaurant, so do you hire a hundred people or ten? You will have some idea. You will know a hundred would be stupid and that ten is about right—how did you know that. You planned it in your head. For a plan to be a plan it does not have to be on paper or in a "fancy" report with charts and graphs—it can be done on the back of a napkin—it is still a plan.

A well-planned business will increase its chances of success. Unfortunately, I don't have statistics to prove that statement; but I sure believe it. Reading this book, I hope you begin to believe it too.

Budgeting

If you hate planning, you are really going to hate budgeting. Budgeting is your business plan with numbers. So now you must estimate everything about the operation of your business and add numbers to those plans. First, of course, is the big one of revenue. Your first attempt at a budget might be to estimate a year.

At this point we need to make a distinction between an existing business and a new business that has not yet opened. Obviously, the process for those two will be different.

Budgeting for an Existing Business

Many business owners will decide after a year or two that they need a budget. Most often that is because they are not making the money that they thought they would and don't know for sure why. Or maybe they are seeking a loan and the lender says they would like to see a detailed forecast for a few years. Either way, you are going to put together a detailed budget for a couple of years or longer. One of the obvious advantages of this process is that the "big" question for a new business is revenue but for an existing business you already have a record of revenue. Now maybe it's not enough and that's what you want to change, but before you can estimate more revenue you have to understand where you are with your current numbers. The budget starts with an analysis of the current operation. This becomes another of those stumbling blocks to a successful business—your numbers are garbage.

I must admit at this point, I am an accountant. Yep, college degree in accounting, CPA, all that nonsense. My bias towards good financial information is real and maybe a bit annoying. But if you want to manage a successful business, you will have to at some point in time rely upon numbers. Bad numbers will generate bad decisions.

If you're not an accountant, you probably should have someone doing your books and giving you financial advice. I know, you can't afford it—but the truth is you cannot afford not to have good financial information. There is a myth in the business world that all you need is a good idea and a willingness to work hard, and you will be successful. There is no doubt that can happen, but if you want to improve your odds of being a success you should pay attention to the numbers. I know it's boring, but the more you know about numbers the better businessperson you will be. But back to budgeting.

If your actual (real) numbers are good that will be the basis of how to put together a forward-looking budget. Otherwise, you guess. That's right you guess. I know many people who hate that, but it should be an educated best guess, not some wild ass dumb guess. The idea of a budget is to document what you think will happen and then compare it with what does. The answer can be "that was a stupid guess." That is part of the process, you will get better at budgeting by doing it.

Budgeting for a New Business

This involves some creative thinking. If you have experience in the industry, you may be able to build a budget by estimating based on your experience. Another approach, and maybe a better one, is to do the research. There is a ton of data available that you can access, sometimes for free, sometimes for a fee, which will give you industry standards for much of the Income Statement categories that would most interest you.

Sticking with our restaurant example, a Google search for average restaurant food costs or restaurant operating expenses brings up thousands of resources for "normal" amounts on a percentage basis. Then the question will be, does your restaurant fall within those "normal" amounts. Normal usually means average and for many reasons your numbers could be below or above average.

To refine your numbers, you may want to contact a trade association in your industry. For restaurants the major trade association is The National Restaurant Association (https:// restaurant.org). Every industry will have groups that represent that industry and act as a clearing house for information about the membership and industry data. More research should direct you to the groups in your industry.

Why Go to All of this Effort?

There are some nerdy accountant types who love to plan, budget, forecast and basically "play" with numbers, but for more normal people this is tedious work; why do it? Success. Understanding the numbers for your industry, planning a budget, analyzing actual numbers compared to industry standards; all of that is to help you be a success. Can you succeed without it—absolutely. But it is harder.

Success in any business is difficult. Small business is the most difficult. The margin for error in most small business ventures is very small. A few bad months and many small businesses will fail. Understanding numbers and knowing how to use that knowledge to your advantage gives you an edge on the path to success. If you can plan effectively, you will have an enhanced chance to reach your goals.

In the next chapters we will cover many subjects involved in planning:

- How do you plan and budget?
- What does it mean?
- Key performance indicators
- The monthly budget process
- The five-year plan
- Review and analysis
- Cash flow plan and analysis
- Revising plans regularly

In my "other" life, I write mystery books. Often those types of books are described as "page turners", no one will describe a book about budgeting and planning as a page turner or exciting unless you think about it as "making money." And making money means a better life for you and your family. Now that is important! Maybe this book is a page turner.

2
How Do You Plan and Budget?

How to Start

Okay, now we think doing planning and budgeting is a good idea, how do we do that? First is having access to a spreadsheet (usually Excel) and a computer. Of course, many plans and budgets have been done without these tools, but it is harder—and you don't want to make it harder.

What should be the first step in planning a new business?

Ran across an article claiming to be offering advice on what you should or shouldn't do to avoid failure in a new small business. One of items was ignoring insurance. Interesting item? Of course, the article was written by an insurance company.

What should you do to avoid failure besides talking to an insurance agent?

Have adequate capital for whatever your business needs will be for at least two years, or even better five. Not sure what percentage of small businesses fail in a year or two almost exclusively because they run out of money, but I would guess it is high. There are stories out there about someone who started a business on 100 bucks and is today a millionaire or even billionaire (the higher number depends on if the story is being told in a bar).

The lack of capital will be the number one reason new businesses fail. Now you could say they lack capital because their business did not generate enough sales. Usually that's not the case. More often it is because the business did have success in sales but ran out of money supporting those sales numbers. When a business is low on cash, the owner will inevitably start making decisions based on the need for cash, not on what the business needs to grow and survive. That spiral downward will often result in failure, even though the business was generating good revenues.

The big culprit in this situation is a lack of planning. Many new business owners will grossly underestimate the amount of capital it will take to start and build a business. And why do new business owners underestimate the capital needed? Because it is hard to figure what you will need, and besides, there is no way they can accumulate that much capital.

Killing your own dream because you can't accumulate five years of working capital at the beginning would take an extraordinary person. It would probably take the type of person who would never risk starting a business in the first place. If you are risk adverse and a detailed planner, you will never reach a comfort level that would allow you to start a new small business.

At this point maybe the question should be what is working capital? Number one—it is not debt. If you started your new business by borrowing from a bank, on your credit cards and kicking in the famous 100 bucks, your working capital is 100 bucks. Often new business owners will consider their available cash through loans as working capital—it is not. It is the opposite of capital. Not only does it have to be paid back, usually on a fixed schedule, but it has a cost—interest.

Okay, sure there was this person who started a business on 100 bucks by maxing out their credit cards and became wealthy. I wouldn't believe those stories. That person, if they exist at all, probably had a rich Daddy or maybe Uncle in the background, who at the last minute kicked in a few grand or a few hundred grand, or if you're a real financial genius, Dad popped for a million. But of course, that fact is usually not in the bar story.

Capital is the engine that drives success in business.

But I have such a great idea? Yep, that has tremendous value. I'm willing to work a million hours a week! Once again, energy, dedication, all have huge business value and can be keys to success. However, the big one is money.

Now, back to the big question; how much capital is enough?

Cop out—*I can't tell you.* It all depends. What type of business, how much in fixed assets, how long before you are generating revenue, how long before profits start, do you extend credit, do you have inventory, is the business seasonal—this list goes on and on.

There are small businesses that can be started on a shoestring, but others require significant capital. The first job is to know how much is required for your type of business. Some of this will just be guess work, some will be research, some will be talking to other business owners; all of it will be planning.

Planning, especially if it involves numbers, is a tough chore for many people.

If you want to reduce the risk of starting a new business, you will have to plan. Plan your first months in business, on paper. Crank up the old spreadsheet and start putting in some estimates of costs over the first year of operation. Those first months will have costs and no revenue. That can add up quickly. Don't make some crazy assumption that you are an immediate success; plan like your idea did not work exactly like you wanted. Then look at those numbers.

Many new small business owners will run through their capital before the doors are opened. Doing the planning with a spreadsheet allows you to make different assumptions which will help you when you start. Look at downsides, what if this can't happen in this timeframe? What does that mean to on-going costs. Don't fool yourself with some ridiculous plan of instant success, such as revenue in the first month at peak capacity. Be conservative with your projections. See what the numbers say.

I think I'm hearing someone say, "if I plan for every contingency and lower revenues, then I would not open my store!" Maybe so. But if you plan for the downside, at least you will not be completely surprised if things do not go as you had hoped.

Make several plans. Best and Worst. High and Low. Look at the assumptions in the plan. It will help you when the numbers become actual.

Just remember, you can never have enough working capital—it is the engine that drives success.

So, Step One should be trying to estimate how much money is going to be needed.

Another way of saying this is to start with the big picture. Look at the big assumptions. How much will it cost to open the doors? How long before revenue begins? How long before I show a profit? How many employees will be required? How much labor before revenues kick in? How much can I borrow? How much will I need to live on before the business starts making money? How many months of outgoing cash flow should I have as a reserve?

Start answering the big questions. Put a pencil to it and figure out what is the range you will need in capital and debt. This process is both the beginning of planning and developing a budget, but also this is the basis of a feasibility analysis. Should I do this?

A self-produced feasibility study has an obvious flaw. You're analyzing you own idea, no doubt, with your own developed numbers. Just a little potential bias built into that approach. Of course, hiring someone to do that kind of study could be expensive, maybe even very expensive. The ultimate feasibility study is done by an independent "professional" with experience in the type of business you are exploring. Once again, big bucks.

So, no reason to spend most of your capital on a feasibility study. Therefore, you go with the "seems okay to me" approach. However, you should attempt your own feasibility study. If for no other reason than what you might discover accidentally when doing the research.

Research

Google until you're blue in the face. It is amazing what you might find just by looking and looking some more. Don't stop at the ten top results—put in the time and effort. Also contact trade associations in your industry. They will often have free stuff that can help you or, in some cases, they sell detail reports about the industry and current trends.

If you have time (and money), you should also consider attending a trade show or conference. Most industries will have a national convention or trade show once a year. There will be people there you can talk to, and you can make a lot of contacts.

Never, ever be afraid to say you don't know. If you ask people for help, you may be surprised how forthcoming some of these resources will be.

Break-Even

Information, facts, data, industry statistics will all have value as you develop your own plan. Even if you have industry experience you should seek out all the data you can find and ask people in your industry for help. Your experience, maybe as an employee, may not have been the best sources of information. Almost all industries will have a range of "typical" performance. You may hear that for your business you can expect gross margins to be between 25% to 55%. That is a vast range. At 25% you go broke, at 55% you may have priced yourself out of a competitive market—and you go broke.

One of the most important analyses you will need to complete is to develop a Break-Even point. This will tell you at what revenue level you will cover all your costs. That is the point where your operation is "breaking-even", not losing money and not making money.

Calculating break-even in theory is an easy analysis, or it can be very complicated. Let's look at a simple example. This is a store front "fast-casual" restaurant. Located in a strip center total square footage is 2500 square feet. (All percentages are just examples. Each restaurant and every industry will have standards that would be objectives, but all industries will have ranges between which it would be "normal" to have such numbers—these are just examples).

Assumptions:

- Variable Labor = 30%
- Food Costs (variable) = 25%
- Variable Overhead = 12%
- Fixed Overhead = $12,000 per month

Break Even = Fixed Costs / Contribution Margin
Contribution Margin = 100% minus (variable expenses/costs)
Contribution Margin = 100% minus (30%+25%+12%) or 33%
Break Even = $12,000 divided by .33,
    or $36,364 revenue per month

Proof:

Revenue		$ 36,364
Cost of Sales:		
	V. Labor (30%)	$ 10,909
	Food Cost (25%)	$ 9,091
Total CoS		$ 20,000
Gross Margin		$ 16,364
Overhead:		
	Fixed	$ 12,000
	Variable (12%)	$ 4,364
Total OH		$ 16,364
Profit (Loss)		**$ 0**

Now that is simple. You can see if all your assumptions about fixed and variable costs are true you will be at break-even doing $36,364 revenue per month. No profit, no loss. Can this get complicated—you bet it can. You can have multiple line items with different variable rates, you can have semi-variable categories, your fixed costs can be fixed up to a point and then jump.

The important thing for now is to understand the basics. Do the simple BE analysis first.

If you know your break-even, the very simple (and very important) feasibility analysis is—*can I do $36,364 sales per month?*

These first steps in planning are just the beginning. As we move forward, we will be discussing more details and specifics about how to plan and budget. However, these first steps are the most critical.

Just doing a simple BE analysis gives you critical information you will need to be successful. You had to think about the elements in your business—what is variable, what is fixed. As you look at each element you start to think as a manager of ways to control those costs and you can see the impact of labor being 30% not 22%.

Another approach with this type of analysis is to forecast sales first. In our restaurant example, we could estimate the number of customers we expect per day and what the average ticket would be. Based on size of the restaurant, hours of operation, location, type of food and many, many other factors you might decide that your average customer count per day would be 110 with an average ticket of $12.50. Which might give you an average month of $41,250 in revenue.

At that point you can do a "reasonableness" determination. Is that a reasonable number? Remember averages can be deceiving, because you will have peaks and valleys that combine to generate the average. Maybe on your good days you must serve 200 customers to offset the slow days. Can you serve 200 customers?

Once you start to develop numbers you can begin the process of analyzing what they mean. Often just good old common sense can tell you something is wrong.

In Chart 1 (on the next page) there is a break-even analysis which we expanded on to look at different revenue assumptions. Our BE point is number 3. Using the same assumptions built into the break-even, we can see what happens to profits or losses with different revenue assumptions.

Obviously, revenue below break-even generates a loss and above a profit. We had previously made a quick analysis that said our average ticket would be $12.50 and we thought are average

Scenario	1		2		3 (break-even)		4		5		6	
Revenue	$	25,000	$	30,000	$	36,364	$	42,000	$	52,000	$	57,000
Labor Variable	$	7,500	$	9,000	$	10,909	$	12,600	$	15,600	$	17,100
Food Costs	$	6,250	$	7,500	$	9,091	$	10,500	$	13,000	$	14,250
Total Cost of Sales	$	13,750	$	16,500	$	20,000	$	23,100	$	28,600	$	31,350
Gross Margin	$	11,250	$	13,500	$	16,364	$	18,900	$	23,400	$	25,650
Fixed Overhead/Labor	$	12,000	$	12,000	$	12,000	$	12,000	$	12,000	$	12,000
Variable Overhead	$	3,000	$	3,600	$	4,364	$	5,040	$	6,240	$	6,840
Total Overhead Expense	$	15,000	$	15,600	$	16,364	$	17,040	$	18,240	$	18,840
Profit (Loss)	$	(3,750)	$	(2,100)	$	0	$	1,860	$	5,160	$	6,810

Chart 1: Break-Even Analysis

customers per day would be 110. Those numbers generated $41,250 in monthly revenue.

We can now see on our expanded chart that $42,000 per month will generate $1,860 in profit. Is that enough profit? We can also see that with an additional $10,000 in revenue we generate $5,160 in profit—a much better number.

This begins the process of developing planning tools to help you access your likelihood of success and what it takes to achieve success.

Just knowing that does not make it happen, but knowing it will allow you to consider if that is reasonable. Before you hardly even get started, you now know you need to generate $45,000 in revenue per month to be even a small "success". You now can analyze that to determine if it is "reasonable".

We might go back to our beginning assumptions and take another look. The average customer count might look too hard to change. 110 per day on average could be the best you think you can do. If your new goal is $45,000 in monthly revenue, you will have to have a higher average ticket price. Your new ticket price target would be $13.60—can that be achieved?

This takes your planning into something that is actionable. Can you raise your price assumptions, can you do combo promotions that will increase the average ticket price, can you expand the menu to increase that ticket price. All these things you can analyze in advance because you did a Break-Even analysis. Planning helps you identify what you need to address and understand about your business before you even start.

3
What Does It Mean?

Before we get too deep into the details of planning and budgeting, we should consider what it means. Is planning the only path to success? Of course not. It is just a tool.

Most new business owners started their journey to being an entrepreneur with a dream. The dream might have been about the business itself or it could have been about the life that could be created as a successful business owner. The dream might have included a new house, a better life for their family, moving to a new town, a feeling of success and importance. All of that is wonderful and those motivations create much of the dynamic of living in a country where you can achieve success on your own. The dream is much more than financial success—it is about each person's desires, both private and public.

That's a lot to pack into a new business venture. Actually, it is too much! All that emotion, those consequential life goals, the commitment to others, your self-esteem—it can become overwhelming. The emotions, the desire for future outcomes take over. You will lose sight of the risks, the downside picture of failure, not only economic, but personally. What if you lose your house due to the business failing—that sure was not in any dream.

Starting a new business, taking the risk, can be the path to a better, more successful life; but it can also be a path towards failure, economic collapse, embarrassment—it can be a disaster.

Planning, especially analytical planning, is meant to remove some of the emotion. "Let's run the numbers", is designed to apply unbiased facts to determine the potential outcomes. It isn't perfect. Mostly because much of what you will be doing is estimating/forecasting/wild ass guessing the future. And even the best "estimator" can make mistakes or use false assumptions. And, if you are doing this analysis yourself, your own biases can influence the analysis with overly positive assumptions.

Planning is only as good as the planner's commitment to research, accuracy, details, facts, and unbiased analysis. You can slant any analysis to prove the point you already had in mind. The hardest part of this process is being honest with yourself. You can run projections using your first assumptions and the numbers can look bad—it is easy to adjust your assumptions with a boost of revenue and now they don't look so bad. But what good is that?

The meaning of the planning and analysis is not to support your business idea, it is to analyze your business proposal to see if it makes economic sense.

In almost all cases it is best to have your analysis and assumptions reviewed by an independent person or even have an independent professional "run" the numbers for you. As I said before, this is usually not done. If a new small business owner plans at all, it is mostly to confirm that their idea is a good one.

The Go/No-Go Decision

Before you invest your life savings, sign the loan papers, or take money from family, you should decide if this is a good idea from a financial perspective. That means developing the analytical tools to decide. Is this a good decision? That is the first meaning of planning. Don't let the dream of success blind you to the risks of failure.

Numbers can help you. The better you become at analyzing business opportunities the better businessperson you will be when those dreams become reality.

At this point you might think I want to turn you into a financial guy like me—I do not. What I want to emphasize is the importance of this type of analysis. Many people can do this themselves, some cannot. If you cannot, you should look for assistance. That doesn't have to be expensive professionals, it might be a family member who can handle a spreadsheet, or a friend who has experience in this type of work.

The other approach is to learn by doing. Make the commitment yourself to understanding the various approaches to developing good analytical tools and learning how to use them. This takes some time, and any many cases will not be an area you will be comfortable with—but analysis can prevent bad decisions. The benefit, besides saving money, is that you will learn the ends and outs of your business. You will be able to see how various aspects of the business fit together. You will learn Key Performance Indicators that will help you manage your business. You will become familiar with statistics that will provide you with the management measures you will need to monitor an on-going business.

What is Different Today

Generational differences exist everywhere. Much of this has to do with communication. There are all sorts of differences with the built-in bias of private knowledge about what certain things mean. Even in business there are attitudes that say, "the old way is obsolete." This has been common with the high-tech industries having so much influence. The OLD business model just does not apply anymore.

There have been high-profile businesses that have achieved

amazing results without making a profit. Some would say the idea of a profit requirement for success is "old school" and no longer applies.

There are three sources of funds to support a business. Investment, loans, and profits. Only one of those comes from the actual operation of the business, profits. The other two are driven by the expectations of profits. To say that it is no longer required to "make a profit", is just wrong. If you can attract investments, especially huge investments, you can sustain a business that is losing money for an extended period. That model can grow a very large base of users/customers which can drive "market value"; but it is still based on the promise of future profits.

If you are starting a small business, more than likely you will not be able to attract large investments. Your survival, almost from day one, depends on being able to generate a profit. This is no different than the business that might have been started by your grandfather. It still requires profits to survive in business.

The New business model and the Old business model still have a lot of common factors. Adequate capital, good business plans, understanding of the operational needs to generate a profit and good management.

This book emphasizes planning as a key to success; but the number one key, as I have mentioned before, is money. Adequate working capital is more important than anything else. The more the better. The reason this is so critical is that it allows you to fail. Yes, Fail. If you have enough money backing your business, you can experience a certain level of failure but still succeed. The money gives you the time and resources to make corrections. We often learn by doing and unfortunately by failing. Using "trial and error" is not something taught at business school, but many businesses work through their first versions to become something different and succeed by employing trial and error. The only problem with trial and error is the cost. Having enough money so that you can fail and try again is often the path to success.

Management

Planning, budgeting, and understanding the numbers is a critical part of management. I've often said, "most small businesses fail due to success not failure." What does that mean? It means many businesses achieve their sales goals, build their customer base, establish their business brand, and still fail—because they did not manage the numbers.

Depending on your type of business, you can fail because you didn't have good control over your assets (inventory, cash, confidential information, customer lists, product detail, sources and much, much more). Control is about understanding the fundamentals of your business. One of the best ways to identify what needs "watching" is by planning. On paper detail your business before you have actual assets and look at what needs to be monitored.

Of course, you can be successful without good controls, or management information, or planning—but it is one of the tools you should master if you want to have a better chance at success.

Can Planning Be Done by Someone Else?

One of the benefits of doing your own planning is that you learn about your business while you are planning. You can build a spreadsheet that reflects your operation and then change numbers and see how they affect the overall operation.

However, if this is something you think you need but cannot do yourself—then by all means consider hiring someone to do this for you.

	Worst		Bad		Not Bad	
Revenue	$ 25,000	100%	$ 30,000	100%	$ 36,500	100%
Cost of Sales	$ 13,750	55%	$ 16,500	55%	$ 20,000	55%
Gross Margin	$ 11,250	45%	$ 13,500	45%	$ 16,500	45%
Op. Exp.	$ 15,000	60%	$ 15,600	52%	$ 16,500	45%
Profit or Loss	$ (3,750)	-15%	$ (2,100)	-7%	$ -	0%

	Better		Best		Hooray!	
Revenue	$ 42,000	100%	$ 52,000	100%	$ 57,000	100%
Cost of Sales	$ 23,100	55%	$ 28,600	55%	$ 31,350	55%
Gross Margin	$ 18,900	45%	$ 23,400	45%	$ 25,650	45%
Op. Exp.	$ 17,040	41%	$ 18,240	35%	$ 18,840	33%
Profit or Loss	$ 1,860	4%	$ 5,160	10%	$ 6,810	12%

Chart 2: Monthly Forecast

Let's look at the simple plan in Chart 2. We have estimated several different revenue levels and used some standard percentages to estimate costs and expenses. For cost of sales, we said that all costs were variable and used some standard percentages we found on the internet. For operating expenses, we fixed a portion of the monthly amount and estimated a variable portion.

This would not have taken a great deal of time. Does this simple forecast tell us something? Of course, it does. We don't have to analyze anything. We can see that below $36,000 per month in revenue is bad and above it gets better. Simple but an important number to know.

If this was the only plan done, it would still be helpful. Obviously, I think the planning should be much more extensive and with greater detail, but don't back off planning because you think it only matters if you have hundreds of pages of planning materials. Do something, it is better than nothing.

From this simple chart we can then ask the critical question; how much revenue can we do? We are a small store, with low overhead; but we are also in a bad location (cheap rent), the restaurant in the same spot went broke, the parking is very limited—some good, a lot bad. Take an honest look at what you think revenue could be. Break it down by customer, average ticket price; make you best guess.

So, if you come up with $30,000 a month is about the best you could do—you don't open in that location. If it looks like $60,000 a month is possible, maybe you jump in with both feet. That is planning. It doesn't have to be elaborate or mind boggling to be useful.

4
Key Performance Indicators

"What is a KPI? KPI stands for key performance indicator, a quantifiable measure of performance over time for a specific objective. KPIs provide targets for teams to shoot for, milestones to gauge progress, and insights that help people across the organization make better decisions." Qlik.com

The most common KPI is sales. Many businesses will get daily sales reports, measuring the progress towards a monthly goal, or compared with previous years. Success in most small businesses is driven by sales. That is a basic, but KPI's can become very specific to your business, broken down by department, by functions, by teams, by locations or by regions. There are many common KPI's, but every business should identify what has meaning for them. Every industry will be different but have some common goals.

Accounting System

The importance of measuring and monitoring cannot be overstated in developing a winning strategy of financial success. To be able to utilize this information in a timely manner you must have a good accounting system. Your accounting system is for your taxes, financials for your banker and other less than thrilling things—but it also drives your information system. Big business spends a huge amount of money on these information systems for one reason—they work.

Small businesspeople will often say "hey, I know what's going on in my business because I'm there every day working hands-on".

That is a valid point. A small business may not need the elaborate systems of a big business, but you better have something. Working hands-on gives your insight a remote manager will never have, but at the same time without data detail, that remote manager may have a better idea how profitable your current operation will be, because he will have reports giving him detail related to costs.

I know this recommendation is going to sound hollow—but you should spend whatever you can afford on a good accounting/information system. Okay, you say you can't afford anything—well then, I would say maybe you shouldn't be opening a business. You must spend some amount, and maybe the most you can afford, to be sure that you have the information tools you will need to effectively manage, otherwise you will be flying blind.

How to Identify KPIs

I think the best approach is to think about your business like it was a large business. Large companies will be broken up into departments, so let's take that same approach for our model small restaurant. What departments will we want to monitor? Food Prep or Kitchen would be one, Personnel or Labor, Sales, or Marketing, and maybe Safety, and then an overall financial view.

The obvious, most important number to most businesses is revenues. A business owner will want to have as much data as possible to able to analyze sales. In our example we have tracked sales based on types of revenues.

The first analysis was Dining and Bar. This includes all revenue for the restaurant captured on where it was ordered. (Another analysis might be Liquor and Food sales). Our budget was a 70/30% split on these revenues but actual was higher sales in Dining versus Bar. Does that tell us anything? Maybe, or maybe not.

	Budget		Actual		Variance	
Dining	$ 36,400	100%	$ 43,150	76%	$ 6,750	
Bar	$ 15,600	55%	$ 13,850	24%	$ (1,750)	
Total	$ 52,000	45%	$ 57,000	100%	$ 5,000	
Take Out	$ 12,500	24%	$ 8,350	15%	$ (4,150)	
Catering	$ 8,500	16%	$ 5,250	9%	$ (3,250)	
Other	$ 31,000	60%	$ 43,400	76%	$ 12,400	
Total	$ 52,000	100%	$ 57,000	100%	$ 5,000	

Chart 3A: Revenue

	Goals		Actual	
	Annual	**Mthly**	**TTM**	**Month**
Sales / sq.ft.	$ 250	$ 20.80	*n/a*	$ 22.80
Revenue per Employee (FTE)	$ 96,000	$ 8,000	*n/a*	$ 8,143

Chart 3B: KPIs

We also captured data for different types of sales, Take Out, Catering and Other. Our budget assumptions had significant revenue contributions from Take Out (24%) and Catering (16%). Our actual numbers were significantly below those targets. Were the budget assumptions wrong or have we failed to emphasize our take-out and catering business to our customers? These numbers would indicate that this is an action item.

One action could be to re-evaluate the budget assumptions in these areas. Did we just guess wrong? This is how you develop a better budget by recognizing the actual world and changing your initial assumptions. (Note: As a business owner/manager you cannot spend all your time with numbers—it would be counterproductive. I'm a strong believer in letting numbers drive your business decisions, however, be sure to control the amount of time you spend on these activities. And if this is not your strength—don't try to teach yourself to be a numbers analyst—delegate, hire someone or at least keep it as simple as possible—you have a business to run, and this is only one of the tools.)

If you still believe your budget assumptions, this analysis will tell you an area that needs attention. Maybe an increase in marketing dollars for these areas, maybe some reshuffling of employee duties to free up time to do catering, maybe a hundred things that can be done to improve this area of revenue.

Other KPI information gives the owner broad measures to see if the business is hitting industry standards, such as Sales Per Sq Foot, or Revenue Per Employee. Revenue per employee would be on a full-time equivalent basis (FTE). In the above example, we don't have annual numbers yet for these KPI's, so it is showing NA (not available). But once we reach twelve months in business, we can track these statistics on a trailing twelve-month basis (TTM). The goals/budget for these types of measures should be based on industry standards. In most industries there will be a range of "normal" numbers based on certain assumptions (size of business is the most common).

If your statistics (KPI's) are either extremely too high or too low, it could be you are comparing apples and oranges. This can happen when you get industry norms, and they reflect different operational realities. The most common is the owner is working many hours per week but taking out very little in salary. Or the other extreme where the owner is not hands-on but taking a salary as a manager. Or maybe Dad owns the building and is not charging you any rent? Remember, the analyzing of numbers is not to win a prize but to give you data that is vital to running a successful business. If you are aware of unusual circumstances that skews your numbers one way or another, you need to make an adjustment to correct the number to a "normal" operation.

Sometime KPI's can seem odd. One that I saw used in an unusual way was shortages or overages for petty cash. Each department in a large company had their own petty cash fund for miscellaneous expenses (often coffee, donuts, and other necessities). Those monies were audited once a month by internal auditors. The CEO of the company ask to start receiving a monthly report on those audits. What had been a relaxed, look the other way attitude regarding shortages took on a whole new importance. Typically, these funds were short because the employees were very relaxed about providing receipts—within months of the CEO making it known he was monitoring this minor asset, the funds balanced every time—and if there was a shortage, an investigation was put in place.

While the petty cash shortage was of no consequence to the company, the importance placed on those funds by their boss caused a new focus on details at all levels of the business. The CEO later claimed, without any support, that his tactic saved the company millions because all employees became super conscience regarding details. I'm not sure how much of that story is true—but what is true, is that what management pays attention to—is what the employees pay attention to.

Another example of a KPI you might not consider is comps in a table service restaurant. Measured as a percent of revenue this can be very meaningful. A comp is a free or reduced-price meal because of poor service or poor food quality. Every restaurant will comp some meals due to some obnoxious customer's demands—easiest path to solving the problem is to comp the meal. So, a standard rate might be 1% to 2% of revenue. While this is a small portion of revenue, it will tell you a lot about the operation of both the front and back areas of the restaurant.

This is also a good example of a KPI that really doesn't tell you what is going on—it is, after all, only a number. But by monitoring this number you can see if there was something unusual on a particular day and ask the questions about what happened.

Every industry/business will have its own sets of KPIs. Every owner/manager will have items that they will want to monitor. These can change, month to month, season to season, department to department. There are no rules here, only the objective of having triggers that will alert you to something that needs to be handled or discussed.

I've had managers tell me they don't need those alerts because they are in the business every day and can see what is going on. There is some truth in that—a hands on manager will have different needs than a remote manager. However, a hands-on manager may be too involved in the workflow and demands of customers to pay much attention to the details. These measures are tools for both hands-on managers and remote managers; you will need to decide what is most useful for you.

5
The Monthly Budget Process

We know that having a boat load of money is the real key to achieving success in a small business, but second on my list is a monthly budget. Okay, maybe that is a little strong, but I'm a big advocate of budgeting. Preparing your budget, forces you to think about the future, think about the variables in your business, think about the things you can control and the things you can't. That planning makes you a better manager. Plus, and it's a big plus, they are your numbers and if you miss them, you must rethink everything built into your assumptions.

In our restaurant budget we planned/budgeted for 25% food costs and 30% labor. If our actual food costs are 27% and our actual labor 34%, we are over our budget by 7 percentage points. Our profit goal was 10% of revenue meaning if all other costs fell in line, we would make just 5% of sales. (Note because our sales were better than Budget our fixed overhead was 22% or revenue compared to 23% in our budget).

The good news in Chart 4 is that you still made a profit of $2,450 or 5% of sales. Plus, your revenues were better than projected. That is all very good news. But you know you must have 10% profit to be successful. At this point you would look at the negatives; food costs were two percentage points higher than budget; direct labor was four percentage points higher.

You were in the restaurant every day, often in the kitchen, you know you could not have handled the business volume with fewer people. Could you pay less? Probably not. So, the labor dollars

	Budget		Actual		Variance	
Revenue	$ 52,000	100%	$ 54,000	100%	$	2,000
Food Costs	$ 13,000	25%	$ 14,750	27%	$	(1,750)
Direct Labor	$ 15,600	30%	$ 18,500	34%	$	(2,900)
Total Direct Costs	$ 28,600	55%	$ 33,250	62%	$	(4,650)
Gross Margin	$ 23,400	45%	$ 20,750	38%	$	2,650
Fixed Overhead	$ 12,000	23%	$ 12,000	22%	$	-
Variable Overhead	$ 6,240	12%	$ 6,300	12%	$	(60)
Total OH Expense	$ 18,240	35%	$ 18,300	34%	$	(60)
Profit (Loss)	$ 5,160	10%	$ 2,450	5%	$	(2,710)

Chart 4: Income Statement, Budget vs. Actual

cannot be cut and still provide the service level you want. How about food costs? You would look at your food cost assumptions, was waste higher than you anticipated, were portions too large, were all orders properly priced on the tickets—after examining everything you might decide that the food costs were not due to error but were actual food costs.

If you can't change costs, you have to look at pricing. You had originally made a significant analysis of the market and competition in your area to determine your item pricing. Raising prices too high will decrease sales, pricing too low will decrease profits—based on your original analysis you thought you had picked the happy medium. Now you need to reevaluate.

Customers want stability, but as an owner you must always be looking at everything in your business and making business decisions when they are necessary. In this case, after a few months, you might examine all items on your menu and re-adjust pricing both up and down with a goal of an overall increase of 5%.

	Budget		Actual		Variance
Revenue	$ 52,000	100%	$ 57,000	100%	$ 5,000
Food Costs	$ 13,000	25%	$ 14,750	26%	$ (1,750)
Direct Labor	$ 15,600	30%	$ 18,500	32%	$ (2,900)
Total Direct Costs	$ 28,600	55%	$ 33,250	58%	$ (4,650)
Gross Margin	$ 23,400	45%	$ 23,750	42%	$ (350)
Fixed Overhead	$ 12,000	23%	$ 12,000	21%	$ -
Variable Overhead	$ 6,240	12%	$ 6,300	11%	$ (60)
Total OH Expense	$ 18,240	35%	$ 18,300	32%	$ (60)
Profit (Loss)	$ 5,160	10%	$ 5,450	10%	$ 290

Chart 5: Income Statement, Budget vs. Actual, 5% price increase

Our food costs and direct labor stayed at the same dollar amounts, so our percentages are lower with our overall 5% price increase. We are now achieving our 10% profit goal.

Obviously, price increases must be done reluctantly and with great thought. Some price increases will result in decreased sales, therefore not creating the result you want. The point of this exercise is to emphasize how planning and budgeting can point you in the right direction to fix a problem.

Changing the Monthly Budget

You have experienced several months of actual operation and it is obvious many of your budget assumptions were wrong. Should you change your budget?

The easy answer is Yes! This is not a contest or a school project, this is your business, your livelihood. You adapt and give yourself the best guidelines you can create. The hard part is that constantly changing tends to lessen the value of the budget.

My advice would be, if a glaring budget assumption is now wrong—change it. If it could be a monthly blip—do not change your assumptions. Also, at least once a quarter, you should rethink your goals. These are your goals, and they are there to help you evaluate the areas where you need to concentrate your time. A well-constructed spreadsheet can simplify these changes. Prepare your worksheet with the idea you will be updating on a regular basis.

One of the areas that has caused me frustration with clients is when the client thinks of their financial information (usually financial statements) as something done for someone else (usually a banker). That is totally wrong. Financial statements, budgets, forecasts, KPI's, variance analysis, all of these are tools for the business owner. As I've said, you cannot become a full-time analyst and I'm sure don't want to be—but a business owner needs to become comfortable with the basics and act based on those numbers.

6

The Five-Year Plan

"My business might not survive for five years why waste my time planning for that long?" Good question. The reason is so your business might survive five years.

Long term planning is a strange animal. It requires the planner to make estimates into the future for a significant period. Of course, everybody knows you cannot predict the future with anything close to great accuracy. So, this is just "guesswork" and meaningless, right?

Yes, it is guessing, but it is guessing with knowledge, and it is NOT meaningless. You are giving yourself a roadmap with details that will help you achieve the success you seek. Planning is a way to look into the future and see what the results might be, along with what the requirements in working capital, future locations, support systems and labor might be. All that gives you a "visual" in numbers on what must happen to achieve that dream.

I've worked with business owners before who when asked to provide an estimate of certain elements in their business (such as revenues) to help build a forecast will make some comment about how stupid they think that is, how could they know what is going to happen? Some of those people succeed in business, but most with that attitude find failure knocking at their door in the near future.

Planning the future, including forecasting financial results, is about the process of developing those future-plans more than making them perfectly accurate. Everybody knows it is just an es-

	Year 1	Year 2	Year 3	Year 4	Year 5
Revenue: Current Location	$ 624,000	$ 686,400	$ 755,040	$ 830,544	$ 913,598
Revenue: Store 2	$ –	$ –	$ 250,000	$ 650,000	$ 682,500
Revenue: Store 3	$ –	$ –	$ –	$ –	$ 350,000
Total Revenue	$ 624,000	$ 686,400	$ 1,005,040	$ 1,480,544	$ 1,946,098
Direct Costs: Food Costs	$ 156,000	$ 13,500	$ 16,364	$ 18,900	$ 23,400
Direct Costs: Direct Labor	$ 187,200	$ 12,000	$ 12,000	$ 12,000	$ 12,000
Total Direct Costs	$ 343,200	$ 3,600	$ 4,364	$ 5,040	$ 6,240
Gross Margin	$ 280,800	$ 15,600	$ 16,364	$ 17,040	$ 18,240
Overhead: Fixed	$ 144,000	$ 144,000	$ 228,000	$ 288,000	$ 384,000
Overhead: Variable	$ 74,880	$ 82,368	$ 120,605	$ 177,665	$ 233,532
Total Overhead	$ 218,880	$ 226,368	$ 348,605	$ 465,665	$ 617,532
Profit (Loss)	$ 61,920	$ 82,512	$ 78,663	$ 200,580	$ 208,212
Percentage	10%	12%	8%	14%	11%

Chart 6: Five-Year Cash Flow Plan

timate. Many future-plans are done based on several sets of assumptions. You might do a five-year plan for both best-case outcomes and worst-case outcomes. Or it might be titled, most-likely or least-likely.

This is not a test of your future predicting abilities but a tool to help you plan for future needs and maybe even spot future problems, long before they happen.

Might be time to address what some of you might be thinking: "I don't have time to do all of this stuff, I have a business to run!"

There is no question this stuff takes time. Is it worth it? You will have to answer that question. Of course, I think it is, but it might not be for you. I would suggest a better question might be, can you afford to not plan and always be dealing with surprises and putting out fires.

If planning is not comfortable, you might consider hiring someone to help. Depending on the size of your business you may already have someone who is more attuned to this working for you. Or if not, you can approach outside sources.

My advice is to try yourself first.

It is possible a more correct labeling would state this as a "dream" rather than a plan. But dreaming is important. We will look at some of the limitations on dreaming this big a little later, but this is a plan of growth and optimism.

What could a five-year plan tell you? Revenue growth has a positive impact—well duh? Opening a new location will have a profit set-back but will add to profits once it matures. Planning on a spreadsheet is quick and easy and totally ignores all the real-world complications about money, time, worry, pressure, bad employees, accidents, customer's demands, and on and on. But it does give you a possible road map to what might be.

An aspect of planning often overlooked is what working

	Year 1		Year 2		Year 3		Year 4		Year 5
Store Capital Investment									
Store 1	$	150,000	$	160,000	$	175,000	$	175,000	$	185,000
Store 2	$	–	$	–	$	150,000	$	150,000	$	175,000
Store 3	$	–	$	–	$	–	$	–	$	200,000
Total Capital Investment	$	150,000	$	160,000	$	325,000	$	325,000	$	560,000
Working Capital									
Store 1	$	25,000	$	30,000	$	40,000	$	45,000	$	55,000
Store 2	$	–	$	–	$	30,000	$	35,000	$	40,000
Store 3	$	–	$	–	$	–	$	–	$	40,000
Total Working Capital	$	25,000	$	30,000	$	70,000	$	80,000	$	135,000
Total Investment	$	175,000	$	190,000	$	395,000	$	405,000	$	695,000

Chart 7: Five-Year CapEx Plan

capital and/or investments are required in the future.

Every business has an on-going need for working capital and investment. The restaurant business is no exception. New equipment, major repairs to old equipment, new signage, updated computer systems—every month there will be something. Often new business owners focus on the up-front investment and ignore the on-going need.

If the business is growing the need for additional working capital will also grow. As we can see in the above chart, the initial investment in our example business was $175,000 and increased each year; and with the assumption of a new store, it jumped dramatically.

Keep in mind this is debt free capital. If the assumption with this model was that the owner invested $75,000 capital and borrowed the additional $100,000—our assumptions are incorrect related to capital. Debt is not the same as capital because it has a cost—interest—and usually a fixed schedule of repayment.

THIS IS IMPORTANT.

The interest on $100,000 debt could be a range of $5,000 to $15,000 per year based on the lowest bank rate and a non-bank lender (credit card?). If we estimated the interest to be $10,000 per year this will change our break-even point for the business. It would increase from our assumption of monthly revenue of $36,364 to $38,887 or a 7 percent increase in revenues to break-even with the interest expense. That is a substantial increase, but probably not a deal killer.

The other important aspect of debt is cash flow. We are going to discuss cash flow a little later with regard to how it can have a

Scenario		(break-even)				(B/E + profit goal)
	1	**2**	**3**	**4**	**5**	
Revenue	$ 36,000	$ 38,887	$ 52,000	$ 57,000	$ 60,915	
Labor Variable	$ 10,800	$ 11,666	$ 15,600	$ 17,100	$ 18,275	
Food Costs	$ 9,000	$ 9,722	$ 13,000	$ 14,250	$ 15,229	
Total Cost of Sales	$ 19,800	$ 21,388	$ 28,600	$ 31,350	$ 33,503	
Gross Margin	$ 16,200	$ 17,499	$ 23,400	$ 25,650	$ 27,412	
Fixed OH/Labor/Debt Pymt.*	$ 12,833	$ 12,833	$ 12,833	$ 12,833	$ 14,125	
Variable Overhead	$ 4,320	$ 4,666	$ 6,240	$ 6,840	$ 7,310	
Total Overhead Expense	$ 17,153	$ 17,499	$ 19,073	$ 19,673	$ 21,435	
Profit (Loss) After Interest	$ (953)	$ 0	$ 4,327	$ 5,977	$ 5,977	
Percentage	-3%	0%	8%	10%	10%	

Chart 8: Break-Even Analysis—Cash Flow Basis

(Debt payment includes principal)*

huge impact on the day-to-day operation. For our purposes here, we can assume that the $100,000 debt is a five-year term loan, and the monthly payment is $2,125 of which $833 is interest. On a cash flow basis our break-even point has increased again to $42,800 revenue per month or a *17% increase* in our previous break-even point.

Because of debt, we went from a break-even revenue number of $36,000 per month to over $42,000 per month. That is break-even, *but our goal was a 10% profit.* To achieve that number and cover our debt payment on a cash flow basis, our monthly revenue number is now $61,000. Of course, if you did not have to borrow money you would not have that issue, or on the other hand if you had to borrow 100% of your "investment" it makes the issue even worse.

This discussion was placed under the five-year plan chapter, but it has impact on every decision you make. Having adequate capital is the most important element in achieving success, not having sufficient capital is often the most important element in failure.

As we "dream" about our five-year plan the capital requirement may be the most critical part. Opening new locations takes capital, running your existing business will take additional capital. Your success depends on that capital and the more you borrow the worse it gets.

7
Review and Analysis

So now you are planning. Preparing a budget, forecasts, and long-term plans. What does it mean? It means you have data to use for analysis to determine if your business is doing what you expected and if there are issues you need to address.

You've done the work of preparing plans, now it is time to compare them to actual numbers and analyze those numbers to see where you can make improvements. At least monthly, you should compare your forecasts/plans to actual numbers for that month. At each monthly review you should also make any changes that are needed to your planning worksheets. As you become familiar with planning and your actual numbers, there may be some obvious adjustments that need to be made. Do it. This is not a test, there are no wrong answers, just data that helps you succeed in your business.

Income Statement (Profit & Loss Statement)

Most every business owner is familiar with the Income Statement. This tells you if you made a profit or not. These statements can be summarized and be simple or they can be extensive with detail regarding sales, cost of sales and expenses. Your planning/budgeting should match up with the same detail as your financial statement. Each line item on your financial statement should have a budget amount.

Sales Reporting

There are exceptions but, in most cases, sales data is the most vital to a successful business—it all starts with that top line. While this is not usually listed as a critical analysis report, it should be. This can be simple or have extensive detail. That will depend on your accounting system and your commitment to implementing the procedures to gather this data.

For our example we were looking at tracking sales by areas in the restaurant and also by categories of type of customers (catering, take out); of course, depending once again on your industry, this can be an elaborate amount of detail related to all sorts a characteristic of the revenue, such as by state, by customer, by sales person, by product, by manufacturer, by time of day, by delivery truck, by department, by store, by source of order—just about any way you can collect and breakdown sales can be a benefit to the analysis.

This is more than curiosity, the more you know about revenue the better you can allocate resources. Most business owners can never get too much sales data.

The same detail can be developed with expenses and costs resulting in P&Ls for various segments of the business. This, however, becomes much more complicated and is usually only done by large companies with an internal accounting staff.

Balance Sheet

This report shows you your assets and liabilities. The difference between those is the equity in your business. Balance sheet measures tend to be used more by larger operations, but this is another tool that should be understood by every businessperson.

Cash Flow Statement

Cash is the most critical asset in a business—it's not your trucks, or your new grill, or your welding equipment—it is cash. A well-designed cash flow statement can be the most important tool you need to manage a successful business. I have designed monthly cash flow statements that not only show where the cash came from and how it was used that month, but also showed the next month's projections.

This is a very simple report (based on our small restaurant model)—it is your check book plus some minor cash items. The report is just to highlight where you are regarding cash. The estimated numbers become more routine once you do this for a while.

This report gives you the heads-up regarding your cash needs as of right now. You do not want to be surprised. You will be out of cash next month. Not to have planned on how you are going to deal with that, could be disastrous.

Reviewing and analysis is not just about profitability—it is also about having the resources your business will need in both the short-term and long-term. Everything about planning is to be able to anticipate and avoid ugly surprises.

Cash balance from previous month	$	**8,250**
Inflows:		
Cash Sales	$	3,500
Collection of Credit Sales from previous periods	$	-
Collection of Credit Sales from this period	$	-
Other Cash inflow	$	-
Refunds from vendors	$	-
Miscellaneous	$	-
Total inflows	$	3,500
Outgoing Cash		
Checks - Payroll	$	4,580
Checks - Expenses	$	2,230
Checks - Other	$	-
Total Checks Issued	$	6,810
Cash Payouts - Labor	$	-
Cash Payouts - Miscellaneous	$	-
Total Outgoing Cash	$	6,810
Ending Cash Balance	$	**4,940**
Next Month (Estimates)		
Estimated Inflows	$	11,500
Estimated Outflows - Payroll	$	3,250
Estimated Outflows - Expenses	$	12,450
Estimated Outflows - CapEx	$	-
Estimated Outflows - Other	$	-
Total Estimated Outflows	$	15,700
Ending Cash Balance	$	**740**

Chart 9: Statement of Cash Flows

8
Cash Flow Plan and Analysis

Understanding the difference between cash and accrual accounting is a critical bit of knowledge that is very important in understanding how to analyze financial data. To reflect the financial results of a business, you must use accrual accounting. Cash accounting only tells you where your cash went and where it came from—is does not reflect profit or loss in your business.

Now, understanding cash is critical to success, but it is not a financial tool you would use to determine the profitability of your business. Both approaches are important, but they do different things.

As an example, let's walk through the first three months of a new business. Don't get bogged down on whether this represents a "real" situation or not—because it does not. We are going to open a business, and in one month have it operational. That seldom would happen, it could be six months or more of pre-opening expenses before you generate a dime in revenue—but just to keep this simple we are only looking at a few months.

In this case the owner is investing \$15,000 immediately and places it into the bank. The first month is spent getting ready with some expenses such as rent, a deposit, some purchased equipment to install and some non-employee casual labor (yes, yes, I know not reality—but the point will be made). This month is getting ready, so no revenue.

On a cash basis all items paid in cash are the expenses and with no revenue, those total amounts are the loss for the month—in

	Cash	Non-Cash	Cash Basis Profit or Loss	Accrual Basis Profit or Loss
Initial investment	$ 15,000			
First Month				
Purchased Equipment *	$ (2,250)		$ (2,250)	$ (62)
Paid Rent	$ (1,250)		$ (1,250)	$ (1,250)
Paid Deposit **	$ (2,500)		$ (2,500)	$ -
Paid Casual Labor	$ (750)		$ (750)	$ (750)
Total	$ (6,750)		$ (6,750)	$ (2,062)
Cash Balance	$ 8,250			
Income	$ -		$ -	$ -
Profit or Loss			$ (6,750)	$ (2,062)

Chart 10: Accrual vs. Cash Basis Accounting, First Month

** This item is a capital expense. In the Accrual method, it is spread across the life of the assets, in this case 36mo.*

*** In the Accrual method, this is a non–expense item, since it will be refunded.*

Second Month	Cash	Non-Cash	Cash Basis Profit or Loss	Accrual Basis Profit or Loss
Paid Rent	$ (1,250)		$ (1,250)	$ (1,250)
Paid Wages	$ (4,580)		$ (4,580)	$ (4,580)
Paid Advertising	$ (980)		$ (980)	$ (980)
Received Bill (Food + Supplies) *		$ 8,400		$ (800)
Total	$ (6,810)		$ (6,810)	$ (7,610)
Cash Income	$ 3,500		$ 3,500	$ 3,500
Income on Credit		$ 1,500		$ 1,500
Cash Balance	$ 4,940			
Profit or Loss			$ (3,310)	$ (2,610)

Chart 11: Accrual vs. Cash Basis Accounting, Second Month

** In the Accrual method, the expense portion is for items used during that month.*

Most of the items represented by the bill were still in inventory at the end of the month.

this case $6,750 in loss. This is what cash accounting does. It records the flow of cash in and cash out—the difference is either a profit or a loss. Accrual accounting is an attempt to recognize what is an expense or income for a particular period and to match those costs and revenues for that period. This method's goal is to as accurately as possible identify a profit or loss for a particular period—usually a month or a year.

With the accrual method our accounting says we lost $2,062 for this first month compared to the $6,750 on a cash basis. We still had no revenue but some of our expenses were either for assets or they did not impact this period in total. Our equipment purchase was for equipment we expect to last 36 months, so rather than showing the total as an expense for this month, we will show only one thirty-sixth of that amount as a monthly expense. The $2,500 refundable deposit which was "expensed" in the cash statement will now be considered an asset and will not impact the Income Statement at all.

In our second month we are now open and generating revenue. This month we paid rent and wages and some advertising supporting the opening of the store. We also purchased a large amount of food items to establish our inventory. Revenue was both cash and credit. On a cash basis our loss was $3,310 while on an accrual basis it was $2,610. Big differences were the food bill and credit income. On a cash basis we did not recognize any food costs because we did not use cash to purchase those items. While on an accrual basis, we took inventory at the end of the month and compared it with the beginning inventory plus the purchase items and determine what the difference was and that was our cost of food for the month. This also resulted in a new asset of inventory. For the cash basis we did not count the $1,500 we sold on credit—we will count that when we collect it. That is accounted for in

Third Month	Cash	Non-Cash	Cash Basis Profit or Loss		Accrual Basis Profit or Loss	
Paid previous month's food bill *	$ (8,400)		$	(8,400)	$	(2,675)
Received this month's food bill		$ 2,450				
Paid Rent	$ (1,250)		$	(1,250)	$	(1,250)
Paid Wages	$ (3,250)		$	(3,250)	$	(3,250)
Paid six months insurance **	$ (2,800)		$	(2,800)	$	(467)
Total	$ (15,700)					
Cash Income	$ 10,500		$	10,500	$	10,500
Income collected from prev. mo.	$ 1,000		$	1,000		
Income on credit		$ 2,250			$	2,250
Cash Balance	$ 740					
Profit or Loss			$	(4,200)	$	5,108

Chart 12: Accrual vs. Cash Basis Accounting, Third Month

* In the Accrual method, the amount of inventory gone for the month is the recorded cost for the month.

** In the Accrual method, the six months are accounted for one month at a time.

Assets		
Cash	$	740
Accounts Receivable	$	2,750
Inventory	$	7,375
Deposit	$	2,500
Prepaid Insurance	$	2,333
Equipment	$	2,188
Total Assets	**$**	**17,886**
Liabilities and Equity		
Liability - Food Bill	$	(2,450)
Equity	$	(15,000)
Profit	$	(436)
Total Liabilities and Equity	**$**	**(17,886)**

Chart 13: Balance Sheet—Accrual Method

the accrual method.

In the third month the differences between cash and accrual are more dramatic. For the month on an accrual basis, we made a profit of $5,108 which was terrific, but on a cash basis we lost $4,200, not terrific. We now see the cash basis is only tracking cash; our loss for the three months is our net cash amount (Income collected minus cash spent). That information is, of course, important—as we see we are out of cash and probably will need to borrow money to keep the doors open.

But the actual financial performance of the store shows a slight profit of $436 but is on a great trend with a fantastic last month. Two different pictures of the same business.

Why the big difference— assets. We used a lot of our cash to acquire assets that will benefit the business for many months, not just these three.

Assets

Cash	$	740
Accounts Receivable	$	-
Inventory	$	-
Deposit	$	-
Prepaid Insurance	$	-
Equipment	$	-
Total Assets	$	**740**

Liabilities and Equity

Liability - Food Bill	$	-
Equity	$	(15,000)
Loss	$	14,260
Total Liabilities and Equity	$	**(740)**

Chart 14: Balance Sheet—Cash Method

While we are cash poor and need immediate infusion of cash, we have accumulated assets. Customers owe us money, we have significant inventory, we bought some equipment, prepaid insurance for the next few months and made a deposit with our landlord.

This is reflected on our balance sheet with a list of money owed (liabilities) and our equity.

As we can see above our balance sheet on a cash basis does not reflect those assets as we expensed them all.

You might be wondering if maybe the cash basis would be better for taxes since in one we made a profit (even though small) and in the cash method we had a substantial loss. Well, you would be correct, and this is allowed. You can use a cash basis of accounting for taxes, but you should use an accrual basis to analyze and understand the financial aspects of your business. So, both methods can be used to your benefit.

We have looked at these differences, so we can discuss preparing a Cash Flow Plan. Cash is King. Cash is survival. Cash is all that matters! Well that last one is a bit exaggerated. But cash, or the lack of cash, is often the main reason businesses go out of business. As I have said before, you can be achieving your business goals but run out of cash and end up closing the business. Many new business owners do not understand the importance of cash and how cash flow is different than the Income Statement. Long-term you must make a profit to survive, short-term your most pressing problem often becomes having sufficient cash to make payroll. Why?

To see why we will put together a Cash Flow Plan. This will include our plan for capital expenditures—a major piece of many businesses cash requirements is purchasing equipment to maintain their operation. These costs are often referred to as CapEx.

This cash flow plan is different than the model we just looked at. To keep things simple the first example made the bold assumption that the total cost of capex was $2,250. The only way that might happen was if the property owner had an operational restaurant which was for lease. That can happen, but typically the new restaurant will need to build out a kitchen and do leasehold improvements. Our cash flow model assumes that it will require substantial investment to open this restaurant. Plus, we are going to assume that we open a second location in year 3.

So, we have gone from a $15,000 initial investment as a leap of faith to our analysis that it will require a $359,500 investment to open two restaurants over a three-year period. As I mentioned, the previous example was based on having an "opportunity" to lease a space that already had existing equipment and leasehold

	Year 1	Year 2	Year 3	Total
CapEx				
Kitchen Equipment	$ 65,500	$ 5,000	$ 2,500	$ 73,000
Leasehold Imprvmnts.	$ 38,500	$ -	$ 3,050	$ 41,550
Fixtures, Furniture	$ 28,500	$ -	$ 5,000	$ 33,500
New Location	$ -	$ -	$ 150,000	$ 150,000
Dining Room Rplcmts.	$ -	$ 1,500	$ 1,500	$ 3,000
IT equipment	$ 3,800	$ 1,500	$ 450	$ 5,750
Software	$ 1,700	$ -	$ 500	$ 2,200
Signage	$ 6,500	$ 1,500	$ 500	$ 8,500
Storage Equipment	$ 5,500	$ 500	$ 1,500	$ 7,500
Total CapEx	**$ 150,000**	**$ 10,000**	**$ 165,000**	**$ 325,000**
Working Capital Estimate				
Cash Reserve	$ 5,000	$ 2,500	$ 5,000	$ 12,500
Customer Receivables	$ 2,500	$ 1,000	$ 3,000	$ 6,500
Inventory	$ 4,000	$ 1,500	$ 5,500	$ 11,000
Deposits	$ 3,000	$ 500	$ 3,500	$ 7,000
Prepaid Expenses	$ 2,500	$ 500	$ 3,000	$ 6,000
Advances on Wages	$ 500	$ 500	$ 2,000	$ 3,000
Total Current Assets	$ 17,500	$ 6,500	$ 22,000	$ 46,000
Accounts Payable	$ 3,000	$ 1,000	$ 3,500	$ 7,500
Other Payables	$ 1,500	$ 500	$ 2,000	$ 4,000
Total Curr. Liabilities	$ 4,500	$ 1,500	$ 5,500	$ 11,500
Net Working Cap. Est.	**$ 13,000**	**$ 5,000**	**$ 16,500**	**$ 34,500**
Capital Requirement	**$ 163,000**	**$ 15,000**	**$ 181,500**	**$ 359,500**

Chart 15: Capital Requirement Plan

improvements. This example requires the owner to provide everything to finish the space and build out the kitchen.

As odd as it might sound, both scenarios would have potentially the same operational results. The first one with little investment could have the same revenue as the second one. The problem with that model is that it is based on being able to find a location where a previous restaurant existed, and the landlord is willing to rent it out cheap—that plan has many requirements you would not control.

Planning involves looking at all your assumptions and determining if they are valid. If your goal is to open a business on a "shoestring", you will have to have a boat load of luck to survive, and more luck to succeed. Money is the engine that drives success. In our first example, the business had spent the entire investment of $15,000 within three months and was just getting started. In the fourth month you cannot pay the rent—your growing business may be over before it even starts.

Realizing this by planning might help avoid a bad outcome.

If you look at the second plan and that is what you want to do AND you have that much money available—your chances of success go up dramatically. If you look at the $360,000 required and all you have is $15,000—stop. You cannot be a success without capital. If you look at borrowing $300,000 of that amount on your house or from your family, you may be looking for a new place to live and having horrible family relations.

Planning is a way to identify reality before it bites you. Planning avoids disasters. Now, I know some of you are going to give me the story of the guy who started his business on $500 and now is a millionaire—well good for him. That person was incredibly lucky—there are a lot more stories out there where people started businesses without adequate capital and lost everything.

I don't want to be Mr. Doom and Gloom, I just want to encourage you to plan, and plan some more, before you take the leap.

9
Planning Assumptions

Anyone who is planning anything will have assumptions built into the plan. Business planning for sure makes many (often-bold) assumptions about the future. The first one might be that there will be a future. We don't think about that much, but it is a fact—the first assumption you make about anything occurring in the future is that there will be one. No reason to get too morbid here, but this is important to acknowledge. All our planning is based on built in assumptions about things we don't know for sure.

Our assumptions could be that everything that matters stay about the same, or it could be that all those things change dramatically. Many businesses depend on most things not changing while other businesses are totally dependent on change.

Every business planner will have their own set of assumptions about the future and how it will impact their business venture.

My entrepreneurial activities began in a totally different world. Wal-Mart was just beginning, there was no Home Depot, no internet, no social media, no personal computers, no smart phones—you get the idea. So if you made a business decision to open a hardware store and two years later a Home Depot opened down the street—your assumptions were very wrong. Many, many small retail businesses were wiped out by the expansion of Wal-Mart and I'm sure most of those owners never thought that would happen. Sears was the behemoth retailer at the time, but they seemed to stay more or less in their lane; but Wal-Mart was different; popping up everywhere with prices the small retailer could not match.

I've discussed this planning assumption with businesspeople before who eventually ask, "Well how can you predict something that you don't know anything about?" Of course, the answer is you can't.

Using our small restaurant as an example, many people are attracted to a new restaurant and will often give you a try or two—so in that segment of the industry your issue will be to provide a good product, good service, at a good price and you can build a long-lasting business. But your customer base will try others, just like they tried you once, so they are not locked in. You let your quality fall, or raise your prices too much; you can lose those loyal customers to the next hot thing.

All business decisions come down to evaluating risk. When you start a new business, you will spend some time thinking about the risk of failure. But often the new business owner will let the dream of success override the concern of failure. So how do you measure risk? Yep, planning; and research.

Every industry will have a different risk rate. Most of the statistics available on the likelihood of failure are based on the number one factor in failing—running out of money (capital). Doing research, you should be able to find statistics of failing in your industry.

The small restaurant example has a first-year risk of failure of a whopping 60%. The source of this number is the SBA and banks so it could be higher, probably not lower. Why would you go into a business that has a first-year risk of failure at 60%? There are several reasons, and they contribute to that failure rate being so high.

One is a low entry point. You really can open a small restaurant on a shoestring. The barrier to being in the food business is relatively low, which means there will always be lots of competition. That also means many restaurants almost immediately are short on cash. So, a lot of these businesses fail before they really have time to establish themselves.

Let's contrast that with the most outlandish example of wanting to open a car manufacturing business. The next great electric car. You might estimate the needed capital at $1.2 billion. Just putting a pitch book together could cost many, many thousands of dollars. Everything about your proposal will have to have incredibly detailed plans with extensive support personnel already on-board to help sell the deal. Total upfront costs for months of preplanning could be $25 million. Therefore, the only way you could open a new car company would be to have access from the very beginning to a huge pile of money. This means professionals would be building the case for this business with massive amounts of support data.

Now the car company could also go broke, but it will take a while because of all of the scrutiny on the front-end and the large sums of money involved. It could be that if you could raise $1.2 billion, you don't really need to make a profit to be successful—all you need is the promise of success.

The small restaurant needs success to survive. Usually almost immediately.

This book is about planning. So if your chances of success are small, should you plan for failure? Odd question, but it might make sense to actually do that. This will help you focus on the risks and what your potential loss might be. I know this is not very encouraging.

I've had people tell me that they are investing $15,000 in their new business venture and if it goes bust, they are comfortable losing that amount. It is always more than what you invested.

Most people will not give up on their dream without a fight. You will borrow on credit cards, from family, beg vendors for credit, ask employees to wait an extra week to get a check; only after trying everything you can think of do you cry "Uncle!"

All those maneuvers will add to the loss. A small business venture with an initial capital investment of $15,000 can end up with a total loss of two, three or even ten times that investment. The worst of these outcomes happens when an owner leverages his home to get more money.

Planning can help you set benchmarks that can be a signal it is time to bail. Stubbornness has value in certain endeavors but throwing good money after bad is not a wise business decision. When working with clients I try to help them set those one-year triggers. Maybe it's revenue or profitability; but something that is simple and easily tracked.

If you set a goal of $300,000 revenue in the first twelve months of operation and the actual number was $200,000 you should probably shut it down. Some will say that is giving up—but surviving a bad business decision takes a lot of courage to recognize you made a mistake.

On the other hand, after twelve months your revenue is $275,000. You might want to raise more capital and give yourself more time to achieve your goals. Mostly what I'm saying is to be clear-eyed about your own business and if you can get out of something that is not going to work and "only" lose you initial investment, you could be making the best business decision available. This could allow you to try again in a few years.

Planning, estimating, budgeting, forecasting are all tools to help you make the best business decision to lead to success; or minimizing the loss.

10

Should You Have a Written Business Plan?

The easy answer might be if you want one. I've told many businesspeople that the best reason to write a formal business plan is that it forces you to articulate exactly what you think your business is about. At one time that was one of the first things a banker or a potential investor might ask for—today it is less so. People are less inclined to read long reports of any nature, and usually are looking for only the highlights.

I would tailor any presentation material to the person reading it. Find out what they want, so you can give them a short presentation highlighting what is important. If they are interested and want more information, then you can provide it.

Should you prepare a business plan for yourself? I think you should, but it takes time and effort. The reward is that you learn a lot putting something together and have a clearer picture of what you want to do. It helps you see areas of weaknesses and strengths. The process itself will have value.

I've used the following outline, but you can decide what is important for you and improvise—there is not one required approach to telling your story or describing the nature of your business.

How to Write a Business Plan

The business plan should tell a reader what your business is about—what it does, who are the people behind the business, how it all works and why the business exists. The plan is a tool—like a map. For it to be the most useful, it will set specific goals and objectives.

1. Prepare an outline. The plan should tell your story—it should be kept precise and focused. Number of pages is not important; readability and concise presentation of information are the most important aspects.

- Cover
- Table of Contents
- Executive Summary
- Business Description
- Definition of the Market/Industry
- Description of Products/Services
- Organization and Management
- Marketing and Sales
- Financial

2. Executive Summary. Short concise summary of your plan. This should be written last—this is not the plan—it should not be more than two pages. However, there are some readers of your plan who will only read the Executive Summary—therefore, it is very important that you highlight the key elements of your plan. The primary goal of the executive summary is to have your reader want to learn more.

3. Business Description. This section can contain a mission statement (business purpose) and a vision of the company in the future. Mission statements should not be statements of personal philosophy, but a statement that relates to what the business is supposed to accomplish. This section would contain the business goals and objectives, a brief history of the business and a list of key company employees. A clear statement of the company's potential is a vital part of this section.

- Mission Statement
- Business Goals and Objectives
- History of Business
- Key Employees

4. Definition of the Market. Here you would describe your business industry and its outlook. Define the critical needs of your perceived or existing market. Identify your target market. Provide a general profile of your targeted clients/customers. The share of the market you currently have or expect to have. The reader will want to know how your business is fulfilling the needs of customers within this market.

- Industry Description and Outlook
- Profile of Targeted Clients/Customers
- Market Share Objective

5. Description of Products or Services. Describe your product and/or services. This should contain sufficient detail for your reader to know what you are going to be providing or selling. Explain the competitive advantages in the marketplace. Describe how the product or service meets the needs of the targeted customers. Include price information and how it fits within the competitive market. Include photos, sales material, or drawings.

- Products or Services
- Competitive Position within Market
- Market/Customer needs addressed by Product/Service

- Price Information
- Support Materials

6. Organization and Management. How is the business organized? Provide an organizational chart. Describe the legal structure of your business (sole proprietor, partnership, LLC, Corporation etc.) Describe any special license, registrations or permits that would be required. Provide brief biographical information on each key member of the management team.

- Organizational Chart
- Legal Structure of Business
- Registrations, licenses, permits etc. required by business.
- Biographical information on each key member of management team

7. Marketing and Sales Strategy. Identify and describe your market. Who are your customers and what the demand for your products or services is. Describe your channels of distribution. Describe your sales strategy—utilize the 4P approach:

- Pricing
- Promotions
- Product/Service
- Place

8. Financial Management. For a new business, this section should include:

- Estimate of start-up costs
- Projected balance sheet

- Projected income statement
- Projected cash flow statement

For an existing business, it should include:

- Balance sheets (last 3 years)
- Income statements (last 3 years)
- Cash flow statements (last 3 years)
- Projections

One of the most important aspects of any new business proposal or plan are the projected financials. Everything we have discussed will be an important part of any financial presentation you make to potential investors or bankers. The more you can discuss how those numbers interact, the more capable you will be in discussing the advantages of your business.

11

Summary

Planning your business is thinking about the outcomes in advance. This basic skill is your best tool for reaching success. Don't get me wrong, perfect planning will not change the outcome of a business venture, but it will help you understand what is happening. Knowledge is what drives success.

Very few small businesses owners will do what I'm suggesting. They will say they don't know how to do it, or that it does not matter, and the important thing is their great idea that is going to change the entire industry. Maybe they're right, I hope so.

If the new business idea was like a car, planning would be the undercarriage, the drive shaft, the differential—all that necessary stuff that's mostly hidden and gets dirty, but makes the car go. Owners are more attracted to the shiny outside and the plush seats. They want to sell the sizzle, talk about their great idea. The hard work of putting together all the parts that make the car go is less fun and more hard work.

We have all heard the stories of someone who had a great idea, pitched it to a few people, raised some money and within a short period of time was a huge success. Yes, that does happen; but seldom.

The typical small business start-up is usually under-funded and under financial stress almost from the beginning. If that business experiences setbacks, it often ends in failure.

The best way to minimize that risk is to plan. Plan, budget, do forecasts. Analyze those numbers, make assumptions about what might happen both good and bad and see how that impacts your assumptions. Planning, usually, only costs you time but may save you from costly bad decisions.

What we did not talk about much is how to measure balance sheet performance. These fall into two categories:

- Liquidity Ratios, such as the Current Ratio, which is current assets divided by current liabilities
- Efficiency Ratios. A/R turnover, Inventory turnover and A/P turnover are the most common

These measures can have value related to public companies and making decisions about investment, or to bankers evaluating a prospective loan customer. These are not used that much in small business analysis.

The bonus section of this book is five case studies. There is a narrative and financial analysis with each of these cases. I would hope that you walk through these and make note of how often the same things keep popping up. While businesses are all different with slightly different circumstances in every case there is also much that is the same. To project whether a new business venture is a good idea you must be able to forecast revenue. Forecasting by its nature is difficult to do. Predicting something that is going to happen is the critical talent needed to do any kind of forecasting including financial. If you are too conservative and your numbers look horrible, you will kill any chance of raising money or securing a loan. If you are too optimistic no one will believe those numbers. The trick is to be somewhere in the middle that still pushes the positive. Now if it is your own money, overselling yourself will lead to financial disaster. Keep a level head, but do not be afraid to believe in the upside. There are few risk-adverse people who have invested in their own businesses—if you hate risk, you should look for a good secure job.

I think these case studies do a good job of highlighting many of those concerns.

I often hear people say something along the lines of, I'm not a numbers person. What they are saying is that numbers and the associated work is not something I'm comfortable doing; what is important is to understand the need in a business for this type of analysis. You don't have to do it to be able to take the data and act upon it.

If this is not your strength, then find someone who can help you with this portion of your business.

Something else I wanted to emphasize at the end of the book; debt is not capital. When we are talking about the investment required to open a business, debt can be a piece of that puzzle, but debt comes with attachments. One of course is cost; interest. The other is an obligation to repay the debt, usually on a fixed schedule. Not much in business follows a fixed schedule, but it is hard to get lenders to see the folly in taking money from you this month when you need it and letting you pay in two months when you don't. Debt can help you maximize your capital, but it comes with its own risks.

Does planning and budgeting make you a successful businessperson? Of course not. But, as I have said before, it can't hurt. It takes some time but the more you do this type of analysis the easier it becomes, and it will help you avoid some surprises and can direct you into areas where financial improvement might make you more profitable.

Thanks for reading, I hope it has helped you approach your decisions with more confidence.

Case study #1: Joe's Eats

Joe Smith had been working in small restaurants for several years. He saw the owners make stupid decisions and they still made money. He just knew he would be a success if he opened his own. Joe was not prone to quick decisions, so he had spent months developing a detailed plan. He had worked on his menu, setting prices to meet certain food costs goals, all those plans were put into a binder. He went over everything many times to make sure he had not made a mistake.

He and his wife had some savings. His wife also had a retirement account that she could tap into. Between the cash they had on-hand and the savings and retirement they could put about $35,000 in the business. His wife had a good job so they could scrape by for some months without him earning anything—but only a few months.

Joe had determined that he would need somewhere around $100,000 to open his restaurant. That was based on a location he had already spotted. The location had been a restaurant and now was vacant. He had talked to the property owner and had spent considerable time estimating the cost to refinish the space to what he wanted. He developed an extensive list for equipment, tables and chairs, signage, computers, and all the small stuff you would need to operate a restaurant. He asked the property owner if he would do the refurbishing and up the rent—the property owner said no. "You know there have already been three restaurants in here that didn't make it. They seemed busy, but I guess weren't makin' a profit. Sorry, I'm not interested in putting any more

	Budget		Actual		Variance
Revenue	$ 385,000	100%	$ 475,000	100%	$ 90,000
Food Costs	$ 96,250	25%	$ 115,350	24%	$ (19,100)
Direct Labor	$ 115,500	30%	$ 145,000	31%	$ (29,500)
Total Direct Costs	$ 211,750	55%	$ 260,350	55%	$ (48,600)
Gross Margin	$ 173,250	45%	$ 214,650	45%	$ 41,400
Fixed Overhead	$ 90,000	23%	$ 105,000	22%	$ (15,000)
Variable Overhead	$ 46,200	12%	$ 58,960	12%	$ (12,760)
Total OH Expense	$ 136,200	35%	$ 163,960	35%	$ (27,760)
Profit (Loss)	$ 37,050	10%	$ 50,690	11%	$ 13,640
Taxes	$ 3,705		$ 5,069		
Net Income	$ 33,345		$ 45,621		

Chart 16: Good Joe's Eats—Financial Statement for the twelve months ending on …

money into that space." The property owner walked off.

Joe knew one of the owners of the last restaurant that didn't make it—and he thought he was an idiot. Joe knew he could do better.

Joe went to some banks to see about a loan. They all said no, except for one. He said if Joe would put his house up as collateral, they might be able to do something. Joe didn't want to do that. He talked to his wife, and they decided it was too risky.

Months went by and all Joe could think about was opening his own restaurant. He was miserable. Eventually he and his wife rationalized that there really was very little risk to their house. There was no way that Joe would fail at something he loved so much. Also, even if it did fail, he could get a good job and they could continue to make the payments on the bank loan. They

Beginning Cash	$	-
Investment	$	35,000
Borrowed	$	65,000
Cash Available	**$**	**100,000**
Purchased Equipment/Leasehold Improvements	$	(85,850)
Purchased Inventory	$	(18,900)
Borrowed from Vendors	$	12,250
Borrowed from Taxes	$	9,569
Paid on Loan	$	(11,490)
Paid Deposit/Insurance	$	(6,700)
Profits from Business	$	45,621
Owed from Customers	$	(12,850)
Non-Cash Expenditure-Depreciation	$	6,950
Net Cash Used	$	(61,400)
Cash Balance	**$**	**38,600**

Chart 17: Good Joe's Eats—Cash Analysis

decided to jump in.

This was one of the happiest days of Joe's life.

This case study looks at two very different outcomes for Joe. One is Bad Joe, and one is Good Joe. We will contract these two scenarios to be able to compare how even small changes from the goals of business can have both very positive and extremely negative outcomes.

Let's start with Good Joe.

Joe quickly got the business opened and experienced success above his goal for the first year. Revenue was better than the goal by $90,000, which was the most significant factor in generating profits. His food costs were better by 1 percentage point and his

Assets

Cash	$	38,600
Accounts Receivable	$	12,850
Inventory	$	18,900
Total Current Assets	$	70,350
Equipment/Leasehold Improvement	$	85,850
Depreciation	$	(6,950)
Total Equipment	$	78,900
Deposit	$	2,500
Prepaid Insurance	$	4,200
Total Other Assets	$	6,700
Total Assets	**$**	**155,950**

Liabilities and Equity

Accounts Payable	$	12,250
Taxes Payable	$	5,069
Payroll Taxes Payable	$	4,500
Current Portion Notes Payable-Equipment	$	15,885
Total Current Liabilities	$	37,704
Long-Term Debt	$	37,625
Total Liabilities	$	75,329
Equity	$	35,000
Profit	$	45,621
Total Equity	$	80,621
Total Liabilities and Equity	**$**	**155,950**

Chart 18: Good Joe's Eats—Balance Sheet as of …

labor costs were worse by 1 percentage point. As a result, his gross margin percentage was exactly on goal of 55%. Higher revenue and on goal margins created a better result in gross margin of $41,400. His profit for the year was 11% better than the planned 10% and generated a profit of $50,690 before taxes.

Joe was a smashing success. His wife was happy and so was his banker.

His banker was particularly pleased with his cash position (see previous page) and balance sheet.

After reviewing these financial statements with his banker, the banker actually took him to lunch—he had never done that before. Joe was flying high.

There has been an old saying that bankers will only loan money to people who don't need it. There is some truth in that. Most lenders are risk adverse. And small business loans are risky. The only reason the bank made the loan was that the equity in Joe's house far exceeded the loan amount. No bank would have touched the deal without that collateral (or an SBA guarantee for the bank). The reason is that if the business fails (and a very high number of small businesses fail in their first years) the equipment and leasehold improvements are worthless. It can actually have a negative value in that you might have to pay to have them removed.

On the other side of the small business gap is the fact that many small businesses can make a lot of money in relationship to the investment if they achieve their revenue and cost targets. That is what Good Joe did in this case and everyone is very happy.

We're calling the next set of numbers "Bad Joe's", you could also call it "Sad Joe's". I've lived it several times and have seen it many times—the failure of a small business. The impact can be very dramatic and totally heartbreaking.

In this case Joe failed to achieve his revenue goals by $80,000. He recognizes now that it would take longer to get the customers

	Budget		Actual		Variance
Revenue	$ 385,000	100%	$ 305,000	100%	$ (80,000)
Food Costs	$ 96,250	25%	$ 82,700	27%	$ 13,550
Direct Labor	$ 115,500	30%	$ 95,600	31%	$ 19,900
Total Direct Costs	$ 211,750	55%	$ 178,300	58%	$ 33,450
Gross Margin	$ 173,250	45%	$ 126,700	42%	$ (46,550)
Fixed Overhead	$ 90,000	23%	$ 105,000	34%	$ (15,000)
Variable Overhead	$ 46,200	12%	$ 42,250	14%	$ 3,950
Total OH Expense	$ 136,200	35%	$ 147,250	48%	$ (11,050)
Profit (Loss)	$ 37,050	10%	$ (20,550)	-7%	$ (57,600)
Taxes	$ 3,705		$ -		
Net Income	$ 33,345		$ (20,550)		

Chart 19: Bad Joe's Eats—Financial Statement for the twelve months ending on …

than he had thought. He had three horrible months before things started to kick-in. His plan was too optimistic and he did not allow enough start-up time before revenue began—a common mistake.

Compounding the shortfall in revenue is that his costs were higher than anticipated. Some of this was also caused by optimistic sales projections. Too much staff, too much food (leading to extra waste) all drove the percentages much higher for food costs and labor. Gross Margin was 3 percentage points lower than anticipated. While the number was not all that bad, the effect of the lower revenues made the drop in gross margin dollars very significant. Fixed costs came in higher at $15,000 over budget, just adding to the woes. That was probably a planning error in estimating some of the costs or not including all of the

Beginning Cash	$	-
Investment	$	35,000
Borrowed	$	65,000
Cash Available	**$**	**100,000**
Purchased Equipment/Leasehold Improvements	$	(85,850)
Purchased Inventory	$	(18,900)
Borrowed from Vendors	$	12,250
Borrowed from Taxes	$	3,675
Paid on Loan	$	(11,490)
Paid Deposit/Insurance	$	(6,700)
Profits from Business	$	(20,550)
Owed from Customers	$	(12,850)
Non-Cash Expenditure-Depreciation	$	6,950
Joe borrowed on his credit cards	**$**	**20,000**
Cash Balance	**$**	**(13,465)**

Chart 20: Bad Joe's Eats—Cash Analysis

items that ended up being required. The effect of these bad numbers was a loss of $20,550. A loss Joe could not afford.

Always the ugly side of losing money is *running out of cash.*

Just to keep the doors open Joe maxed out his credit cards and put an additional $20,000 into the business only to have it sucked out almost immediately, leaving him overdrawn at the bank $13,465. The banker said he would have to cover that in two days, or they would close the account and call his loan (meaning taking his house).

The irony was that the last half of the year was looking better. All of the trends were improving with sales in the last two months matching his original estimates.

Assets		
Cash	$	(13,465)
Accounts Receivable	$	12,850
Inventory	$	18,900
Total Current Assets	$	18,285
Equipment/Leasehold Improvement	$	85,850
Depreciation	$	(6,950)
Total Equipment	$	78,900
Deposit	$	2,500
Prepaid Insurance	$	4,200
Total Other Assets	$	6,700
Total Assets	**$**	**103,885**
Liabilities and Equity		
Accounts Payable	$	12,250
Borrowed from Owner—Joe	$	20,000
Payroll Taxes Payable	$	3,675
Current Portion Notes Payable-Equipment	$	15,885
Total Current Liabilities	$	51,810
Long-Term Debt	$	37,625
Total Liabilities	$	89,435
Equity	$	35,000
Profit	$	(20,550)
Total Equity	$	14,450
Total Liabilities and Equity	**$**	**103,885**

Chart 21: Bad Joe's Eats—Balance Sheet as of ...

Joe did not have any good options left. He and his wife fought, and she was threatening to leave—she couldn't take it any longer.

Joe was miserable.

One of the things we discussed at the beginning of this book was the importance of having lots and lots of cash. The more capital you have, the more likely you will succeed. And it is almost always because you can fail and still try again. If Joe had $50,000, he probably would have been a success even with the terrible start to his business. You always need a margin for error.

But Joe doesn't have $50,000 or $20,000, so the most likely outcome is that he loses his house and becomes very bitter. Life sucks.

Does planning stop any of that? Probably not, but it can't hurt. Good planning will give you all the clues about how critical revenue, profits and cash are. If you start a business on a shoestring, you are increasing your risk by some amazing factor. Start with an extra $100,000 in the bank you don't think you'll need, and you increase your chances of success by that same amazing factor. Cash is king.

What Should Joe Have Done?

Okay, having an extra hundred grand is probably not an achievable goal for Joe. The red flags were there, but like many people, Joe decided to risk it. In the "Good Joe" world, it worked. The first year was a huge success and Joe was on top of the world. The risk was worth it.

In the "Bad Joe" world, he has lost his business and his house and is deeply in debt. Bankruptcy is on the horizon. (And as often happens his family life is a mess.) Could he have seen that risk before he jumped in? Of course, but like many before him knowing the high risk is often part of the excitement in starting the business. It's not for everyone but for some it's addictive.

	Mon	Tue	Wed	Thu	Fri	Sat	Sun	Total
Budget Assumes								
Customers	70	60	60	60	125	150	100	625
Average Ticket	$ 8.50	$ 8.50	$ 8.50	$ 12.50	$ 13.50	$ 14.50	$ 12.50	$ 11.21
Revenue	$ 595.00	$ 510.00	$ 510.00	$ 750.00	$ 1687.50	$ 2175.00	$ 1250.00	$ 7477.50
Best Case								
Customers	85	80	80	90	140	160	140	775
Average Ticket	$ 8.50	$ 8.50	$ 8.50	$ 12.50	$ 13.50	$ 14.50	$ 12.50	$ 11.21
Revenue	$ 722.50	$ 680.00	$ 680.00	$ 1125.00	$ 1890.00	$ 2320.00	$ 1750.00	$ 9167.50
Worst Case								
Customers	55	50	50	50	100	120	65	490
Average Ticket	$ 8.50	$ 8.50	$ 8.50	$ 12.50	$ 13.50	$ 14.50	$ 12.50	$ 11.21
Revenue	$ 467.50	$ 425.00	$ 425.00	$ 625.00	$ 1350.00	$ 1740.00	$ 812.50	$ 5845.00

Chart 22: Joe's Revenue Assumptions—Customer Count scenarios

Key Points

Never risk all your capital without a good reserve for an emergency. Joe not only risked all his capital, but he also borrowed money to make it happen. No reserve and debt are asking for trouble. Joe's response would be then I couldn't have opened the business—YES, that is the point. If you only have $35,000 in free capital, you cannot open a business that needs $100,000 or more to be able to operate. If you cover that difference with debt, the risk of going broke goes up exponentially.

Joe might say, "but in the 'Good' scenario, everything worked out and I became a success with only the $35,000." This is correct. That is how people get in trouble. You can put together the numbers that will say this is a good risk to take, when the risk is probably about 80% failure and 20% success. Those are not good odds to risk your house and much more.

The big unknown in planning a new business is revenue. It is vital to spend much of your planning time on estimating revenue, since that will be the largest element in whether you can be successful or not.

If Joe had done this analysis, it might look something like the above charts. Total customers for the week are estimated at 625 with an average ticket price per customer of $11.21. That varies by day mostly because during the week most of his customers are during lunch hours and on weekends it is dinner, which has a higher average ticket price. If that count is higher that is good, lower—that is bad.

So how do you determine what the count will be? You can't. That's right you can't, with absolute accuracy. There are too many variables and unknowns to make a perfect prediction. You can talk to other businesses in the area, maybe even restaurants, and ask them about traffic—often other business owners, even

	Mon	Tue	Wed	Thu	Fri	Sat	Sun	Total
Budget Assumes								
Customers	70	60	60	60	125	150	100	625
Average Ticket	$ 8.50	$ 8.50	$ 8.50	$ 12.50	$ 13.50	$ 14.50	$ 12.50	$ 11.21
Revenue	$ 595.00	$ 510.00	$ 510.00	$ 750.00	$ 1687.50	$ 2175.00	$ 1250.00	$ 7477.50
Best Case								
Customers	70	60	60	60	125	150	100	625
Average Ticket	$ 11.50	$ 11.75	$ 12.00	$ 12.00	$ 15.50	$ 17.50	$ 16.50	$ 13.82
Revenue	$ 805.00	$ 705.00	$ 720.00	$ 720.00	$ 1937.50	$ 2625.00	$ 1650.00	$ 9162.50
Worst Case								
Customers	70	60	60	60	125	150	100	625
Average Ticket	$ 7.50	$ 7.50	$ 7.50	$ 7.50	$ 10.00	$ 11.50	$ 10.00	$ 8.79
Revenue	$ 525.00	$ 450.00	$ 450.00	$ 450.00	$ 1250.00	$ 1725.00	$ 1000.00	$ 5850.00

Chart 23: Joe's Revenue Assumptions—Average Ticket scenarios

competitors, are willing to help. It's a good human quality.

The location Joe chose has been restaurants before—they have failed. If you could find contact info for those people, that could be a great source of data. Maybe they had great traffic and there were other reasons for their failure, or at least you would hope so.

No matter how much research you do this sort of data is still at best just a guess. Locations are often a huge factor in traffic, but circumstances can change. A new road might be taking traffic away from the location, or new shopping areas have developed and reduced the traffic in your location. It is a maze of information that can be daunting, but it should all be explored and then make you best "guess".

If all of your homework says the most traffic you could expect would be about 500 customers per week, then you will definitely pull the plug on this location. Don't fall in love with one spot before you do the research.

Once you've decided that the average number of customers was good based on your budget assumptions, the next thing to look at would be average ticket—or dollar amount of each customer's orders. This is easier to research because you can see you competitors' prices and determine your costs. Based on Joe's calculations his average ticket price needs to be $11.21 to meet his margin goals. That becomes his budget assumptions; are they reasonable?

If you research the market and you are too high, you will have to rethink some of your assumptions. Ideally your desired budget numbers and the market research will indicate your numbers are correct. The average ticket price is much more in your control than customer count. Obviously, you can raise prices, but that can have a negative customer count result; or you could lower prices and hope your average customer count rises.

Doing all of this in advance on a spreadsheet can help you make the decision to move forward. Understanding all of the pieces and how they interact and what you can control and what you can't, will make you a better manager once the business is up and running.

Conclusion

Investing and losing his $35,000 was worth the risk, but borrowing on his house was not. Once Joe saw he could not afford to do this deal without a bunch of debt, he should have backed off. What options did he have? He could have looked for a partner and/or investor. This, of course, can create its own set of problems but without additional money, this was not a good deal.

How about the "Good Joe's Eats" success. Why was that not worth the risk? These types of questions are hard to answer. Obviously, if you believed 100% the first year's results would be the "Good Joe's", go for it. During some of my own experiences, I have tried to apply risk assumptions to various options but there is no way to do that without making many arbitrary assumptions—the risk calculations cannot be accurate because *we do not know the future.*

I would say risking everything and going deeply in debt is too high a burden on most small business ventures. Even if you believed the best results for Joe's, you have to be concerned about the fact that with only limited resources you cannot survive unless everything goes perfectly. Wishing for perfect is not a good business strategy.

According to data from the Bureau of Labor Statistics, approximately twenty percent of small businesses fail within the first year. By the end of the second year, thirty percent of businesses will have failed. By the end of the fifth year, about half will have failed.

That's for all small businesses, how about small restaurants like Joe's?

The National Restaurant Association estimates a thirty percent failure rate in the restaurant industry. In other words, one in three restaurants won't survive their first year.

The most common reason for failure is a lack of cash. The only way to reduce that risk is to not go into a business with only the minimum cash. If you do not have that "extra" cash reserve, continue to save and plan and evaluate until you do. Save your money Joe!

Case study #2: Jane's Yoga Studio

Jane Jones had been an art teacher for many years and being frugal by nature, has managed to save $75,000. She also had a 401k retirement account from her first job as an executive secretary that she could access without penalty of $210,000. Jane loved teaching art but her true passion was yoga. She was going to retire next month and would receive monthly funds from her teachers' pension plan.

She was considering opening a Yoga studio devoted to seniors. Jane was retiring, in her early sixties but thought the yoga for seniors' market was underserved and she believed she had a lot of good ideas on how to attract customers.

She had done some research and had found different rental spaces in her market area. One she thought might be too small, one was about right, but the last one would have great expansion possibilities. They were all basically bare and it would take quite a bit to finish it the way she wanted. She had asked all the property owners about doing the leasehold improvements and including it in the rent—they all said no. But two of them really liked the idea of a senior yoga studio and lowered their asking rent price to entice her into the location.

Jane was excited and eager to get going. But first, she would need to "run the numbers". Jane had never owned her own business but had been reading a lot about how to begin.

Step one, what is it going to cost. There were three options related to cost based on the size of the space. Her first impression was that 2500 square feet was too small and 7500 was too large.

	Option 1	Option 2	Option 3
Size of Space (sq.ft.)	2,500	5,000	7,500
Leasehold Improvement ($10/sq.ft)	$ 25,000	$ 50,000	$ 75,000
Equipment/Chairs/Mats	$ 1,500	$ 2,500	$ 3,500
Coffee kiosk	$ 2,500	$ 2,500	$ 2,500
Signage	$ 3,500	$ 4,500	$ 4,500
Advertising	$ 8,500	$ 8,500	$ 8,500
Web Site	$ 3,500	$ 3,500	$ 3,500
Licensing	$ 1,500	$ 1,500	$ 1,500
Employee Training Mtls.	$ 2,500	$ 2,500	$ 3,500
Computers	$ 3,000	$ 3,000	$ 4,000
Miscellaneous	$ 1,500	$ 1,500	$ 1,500
Washing Equipment	$ 3,500	$ 3,500	$ 3,500
Mirrors	$ 2,000	$ 4,000	$ 6,000
Video/Audio Equipment	$ 3,000	$ 4,000	$ 5,000
Wages Prior to Opening	$ 3,500	$ 3,500	$ 3,500
Total	$ 65,000	$ 95,000	$ 126,000
Working Capital	$ 25,000	$ 25,000	$ 30,000
Total Investment Capital	**$ 90,000**	**$ 120,000**	**$ 156,000**

Chart 24: Jane's Yoga Studio—Initial Investment Analysis

	Option 1	Option 2	Option 3
Total participants—per day	96	144	240
Total participants—per week	576	864	1440
Total participants—per month	2304	3456	5760
Average sessions per month	6	6	6
Number of Clients per month	384	576	960

Chart 25: Jane's Yoga Studio—Customers/Clients Estimates

	Option 1	Option 2	Option 3
Participants & Fees			
Size of Space (sq.ft.)	2,500	5,000	7,500
Rooms	2	3	5
Sessions per Day per Room	4	4	4
Total Sessions per Day	8	12	20
Participants per Session	12	12	12
Total Participants per Day	**96**	**144**	**240**
Fee per Participant	$ 20	$ 20	$ 20
Total Fees per Day	$ 1,920	$ 2,880	$ 4,800
Weekly Fees (6 days)	$ 11,520	$ 17,280	$ 28,800
Monthly Fees (4 weeks)	$ 46,080	$ 69,120	$ 115,200
Rent			
Rent per sq.ft. per Year	$ 30	$ 29	$ 27
Annual Rent	$ 75,000	$ 145,000	$ 202,500
Monthly Rent	$ 6,250	$ 12,083	$ 16,875
Instructors & Wages			
Sessions per day	4	4	4
Number of Instructors	2	3	5
Hostesses	2	3	4
Total Employees	4	6	9
Weekly Wages ($800 ea.)	$ 3,200	$ 4,800	$ 7,200
Monthly Wages (4 wks.)	$ 12,800	$ 19,200	$ 28,800

Chart 26: Jane's Yoga Studio—Revenue and Cost Assumptions
(Continues on next page)

	Option 1		Option 2		Option 3	
Overhead—Monthly						
Utilities	$	1,850	$	2,750	$	4,250
Advertising	$	4,608	$	6,912	$	11,520
Insurance	$	2,500	$	5,000	$	7,500
Web/Internet	$	3,000	$	3,000	$	3,000
Phones	$	1,850	$	2,450	$	3,675
Accounting/Legal	$	1,250	$	1,500	$	2,000
Cleaning	$	2,000	$	3,850	$	6,250
Security/Misc.	$	1,250	$	2,500	$	3,500
Total Overhead	$	18,308	$	27,962	$	41,695
Profit & ROI						
Profit Before Taxes & OC	$	8,722	$	9,875	$	27,830
Annualized	$	104,664	$	118,496	$	333,960
Return on Invested Capital		116%		99%		214%
Owner's Compensation	$	50,000	$	50,000	$	50,000
Profit before taxes, after OC	$	54,664	$	68,496	$	283,960
Return on Invested Capital		61%		57%		182%

Chart 26, Concluded

But she needed to do some more analysis to help her decide. The cost differences were obvious (Chart 24, previous page).

The cost differences were significant considering her amount of capital to invest. She immediately decided the small space was the best option. However, the more she thought about it, she wondered if the other options might not have value. She sure couldn't move after investing so much in leasehold improvements and having a long-term lease. So, if the 2500 size studio was not large enough, there was not much she could do because the spaces on each side were occupied with long-term businesses.

What about profitability for each option? Which was best?

Chart 25 (on page 91) looks at the key (most critical) piece of our analysis—the number of customers/clients. This is a service business that is 100% dependent on its "in-store" customer base for revenue. There could be product sales but for this example we are assuming all revenue is fee revenue. No outside/internet sales, only studio visitors generating revenue.

How many customers can you attract to enroll in a class? Option 1 says our target is 96 paying customers per day, or 576 week or 2,304 for a month—but most of those customers will visit more than once a month. We will guess that on average each customer will visit 6 times a month. That would mean we would need 384 unique customers for the month. For option 2 that number is 576 and option 3 is 960. Now are those reasonable numbers?

Once again this is the hard part, how do you determine what is reasonable related to revenue projections.

Jane's opinion was that she had been in the town for many years and knew many people, including all the older members of the large church she attended. Also, she had planned on spending $8,500 in start-up advertising—so she thought she could achieve those numbers. Of course, she understood the huge difference between 960 and 384.

So, what does that mean in terms of profitability?

Jane had done research and determined she would be within the existing market charging $20 per session. Using the previously developed customer numbers, she developed a revenue and cost assumption schedule (Chart 26, previous page).

Monthly		
Rent Fixed	$	6,300
Other Fixed Overhead	$	14,000
Fixed Wages (including owner)	$	9,200
Total Fixed	$	29,500
Variable		
Variable Overhead		6.5%
Variable Wages		18.0%
Total Variable		24.5%
Break-Even Calculation		
Total fixed costs	$	$29,500
Total variable costs		24.5%
100% minus variable costs		75.5%
Fixed divided by (100%-variable)		$29,500÷75.5%
Monthly Break-even	$	**39,073**
Proof		
Revenue	$	39,073
Fixed Expenses	$	29,500
Variable Overhead	$	2,540
Variable Wages	$	7,033
Total Expenses	$	39,073
Profit/Loss	$	-

Chart 27: Jane's Yoga—Break-Even Analysis

At those assumption levels for customers and fees each option was profitable. After compensation for Jane, the first option would generate $54,664 in pre-tax profit, the second option was $68,496 and the third option was $283,960 (which was almost unbelievable).

To help her understand how the numbers worked together, she did a break-even analysis (Chart 27, previous page).

Jane was surprised that the break-even was so close to her Option #1, and she thought Option #1 was terrific. Why was the difference so small? Jane's business is a service business with labor and overhead being the majority of costs/expenses. Also, a service business such as Jane's will have fairly high fixed expenses (rent, insurance, utilities, phones, base labor, owners comp) compared to low variable expenses—total variable is 24.5% of revenue. This means once you cover the fixed expenses for the month the additional revenue is very profitable. Or said another way, once you reach break-even every dollar beyond that will generate 75.5% profit. Now that does not work forever. There will be plateaus where additional revenue will require additional fixed costs, but generally speaking, once a service business covers fixed costs profits are high. The revenue projected for one month of $46,080 is $7,000 above break-even and 75% of that would be profits.

Jane is starting to feel comfortable with the prospects for her new business. After some struggle with the tempting bigger numbers for option 3, she was sure that would not be her best choice. While the return on investment would be fantastic, getting that many customers (approaching 1,000) felt very risky. She was still nervous about getting almost 400. Option 3 was out.

Option 2 had some pluses but the profits in the bigger space were not that much better than option 1 and the customer numbers still had her worried.

She knew she had sufficient capital to even absorb a period of loss with option 1 and if it was a success, it would also contribute a very good return on her investment. She decided option 1 was

	Option 1		Actual
Size of Space (sq.ft.)		2,500	2,500
Leasehold Improvement	$	25,000	$ 32,980
Equipment/Chairs/Mats	$	1,500	$ 1,250
Coffee kiosk	$	2,500	$ 1,490
Signage	$	3,500	$ 3,800
Advertising	$	8,500	$ 11,000
Web Site	$	3,500	$ 2,500
Licensing	$	1,500	$ 1,850
Employee Training Mtls.	$	2,500	$ 2,300
Computers	$	3,000	$ 3,500
Miscellaneous	$	1,500	$ 2,000
Washing Equipment	$	3,500	$ 2,875
Mirrors	$	2,000	$ 2,000
Video/Audio Equipment	$	3,000	$ 3,000
Wages Prior to Opening	$	3,500	$ 4,500
Total	$	65,000	$ 75,045
Working Capital	$	25,000	$ 25,000
Total Investment Capital	**$**	**90,000**	**$ 100,045**

Chart 28: Jane's Yoga Studio—Investment Analysis, Year 1

her best choice. She moved forward and signed the lease.

Now it is one year later, and Jane has actual numbers to analyze. How does it look? (See Chart 28.)

She spent about $10,000 more than she had planned. By far the majority of that was in leasehold improvements. Everything just cost a bit more than she had anticipated. While the $10,000 was not a small amount, she was not displeased. She now realizes

	Option 1		Actual
Participants & Fees			
Size of Space (sq.ft.)	2,500		5,000
Rooms	2		2
Sessions per Day per Room	4		4
Total Sessions per Day	8		8
Participants per Session	12		11
Total Participants per Day	**96**		**88**
Fee per Participant	$ 20	$	18.50
Total Fees per Day	$ 1,920	$	1,628
Weekly Fees (6 days)	$ 11,520	$	9,768
Monthly Fees (4 weeks)	$ 46,080	$	39,072
Rent			
Rent per sq.ft. per Year	$ 30	$	30
Annual Rent	$ 75,000	$	75,000
Monthly Rent	$ 6,250	$	6,250
Instructors & Wages			
Sessions per day	4		4
Number of Instructors	2		2
Hostesses	2		3
Total Employees	4		5
Weekly Wages ($800 ea.)	$ 3,200	$	4,000
Monthly Wages (4 wks.)	$ 12,800	$	16,000

Chart 29: Jane's Yoga—Revenue and Cost, Assumptions vs. Actual
(Continues on next page)

	Option 1	Actual
Overhead—Monthly		
Utilities	$ 1,850	$ 1,875
Advertising	$ 4,608	$ 4,500
Insurance	$ 2,500	$ 2,500
Web/Internet	$ 3,000	$ 2,750
Phones	$ 1,850	$ 1,800
Accounting/Legal	$ 1,250	$ 1,250
Cleaning	$ 2,000	$ 1,800
Security/Misc.	$ 1,250	$ 1,850
Total Overhead	$ 18,308	$ 18,325
Profit & ROI		
Profit Before Taxes & OC	$ 8,722	$ (1,503)
Annualized	$ 104,664	$ (18,036)
Return on Invested Capital	116%	-18%
Owner's Compensation	$ 50,000	$ 50,000
Profit before taxes, after OC	$ 54,664	$ (68,036)
Return on Invested Capital	61%	-68%

Chart 29, Concluded

she could have missed her target by a whole lot more—the number of surprises was amazing.

Actual results were the infamous good news—bad news combination (Chart 29). Overall results in revenue were right at her break-even number, but there was a loss because she had added some fixed overhead. She had ended up employing an extra person over what she had initially thought—even though

	Year 1 Actual	Year 2 Budget
Participants & Fees		
Size of Space (sq.ft.)	2,500	5,000
Rooms	2	2
Sessions per Day per Room	4	4
Total Sessions per Day	8	8
Participants per Session	11	11
Total Participants per Day	**88**	**88**
Fee per Participant	$ 18.50	$ 20
Total Fees per Day	$ 1,628	$ 1,760
Weekly Fees (6 days)	$ 9,768	$ 10,560
Monthly Fees (4 weeks)	$ 39,072	$ 42,240
Rent		
Rent per sq.ft. per Year	$ 30	$ 30
Annual Rent	$ 75,000	$ 75,000
Monthly Rent	$ 6,250	$ 6,250
Instructors & Wages		
Sessions per day	4	4
Number of Instructors	2	2
Hostesses	3	2.5
Total Employees	5	4.5
Weekly Wages ($800 ea.)	$ 4,000	$ 3,600
Monthly Wages (4 wks.)	$ 16,000	$ 14,400

Chart 30: Jane's Yoga—Revenue and Cost, Year 1 + Year 2 Budget
(Continues on next page)

	Option 1	Actual
Overhead—Monthly		
Utilities	$ 1,875	$ 1,875
Advertising	$ 4,500	$ 2,500
Insurance	$ 2,500	$ 2,500
Web/Internet	$ 2,750	$ 2,750
Phones	$ 1,800	$ 1,800
Accounting/Legal	$ 1,250	$ 1,250
Cleaning	$ 1,800	$ 1,800
Security/Misc.	$ 1,850	$ 1,850
Total Overhead	$ 18,325	$ 16,325
Profit & ROI		
Profit Before Taxes & OC	$ (1,503)	$ 5,265
Annualized	$ (18,036)	$ 63,180
Owner's Compensation	$ 50,000	$ 50,000
Profit before taxes, after OC	$ (68,036)	$ 13,180

Chart 30, Concluded

customer numbers were in the range of her estimate—it just took more people to manage those customers than she had anticipated. Still, many of the assumptions were in the ballpark. She was not completely disappointed but realized that if she did not have a little extra capital this could be a back breaker.

One of the issues with the first year is that she gave way too many discounts to new customers. While it seemed to work, she now felt going forward with good reviews and word-of-mouth she would not have to do that so much. She believes in the second year she could get the average fee up to the original $20.

Also, hiring the additional host might have been an overreaction to workload. As the year progressed, she could see they could manage with only a part-timer in that position. Two of her full-times decided they would like to work part-time so she could keep them but cut costs by one-half an employee. Also, there were some adjustments in costs that she could make.

Her second-year plan (Chart 30) was now showing a wonderful profit while paying her the comp she wanted. She was much more confident in her planning for that year than before—she had learned a lot.

One of the important aspects of planning is that you become much better at making adjustments as you get actual results.

Jane had $75,000 cash and $210,000 in retirement savings. Her plan was to spend $90,000 to start the business. She had hoped the business could supplement her income by $50,000 in the first year.

What really happened? The initial investment was $10,000 more than planned. The business did not make enough to pay Jane anything and there was a loss Jane had to cover. Meaning that rather than the $90,000 Jane planned to invest, she ended up investing about $170,000—which was $80,000 more than she had anticipated.

Jane had the money and can do that so the business will continue. Also, she is comfortable that a few changes will make the business profitable and be able to pay her. From her original capital she is down to about $115,000 left in her retirement account. She does not have the capital to fully fund another loss year.

This is an area where sometimes things get a little confusing. There are people who invest in a business and expect to work and to take out a salary. But they don't work that hard and the business could probably run itself. We're not sure if that is true about Jane. But let's make the bold assumption that Jane is helping the business but not overly critical to the operation. Then you would look only at the loss of $18,000 and not include Jane's comp in the loss. Her additional investment would then be only $30,000 more than the $90,000 she expected. And (and this is important) her return in the second year is $63,000 profit off of her investment of $120,000 is very impressive.

Small business analysis is driven very much by how the owner treats their compensation and how critical their involvement is to the success of the business.

The contrasts between Joe's circumstances and Jane's after one year should highlight the importance of capital. Bad Joe's first year had a loss very similar to Jane's, but that loss brought Joe to the verge of bankruptcy verses Jane's first year loss being an adjustment year to "hopefully" have a profitable second year—because she had that "extra" capital to absorb the loss.

In Bad Joe's case he has also lost control of the decision about whether to stay open or close his business. Because he chose a path involving debt, his banker will now make the decision about Joe's future—and the banker will be making that decision to benefit the bank not Joe.

On the other hand, if "Good Joe" had happened, Joe would be smiling big. He would have taken a huge risk and won. I would never tell anyone the risk is not worth it, but I sure would want them to understand what failure means to them and their family. There are almost no small business ventures that are not risky, it is just a matter of knowing about the risk and making sure you can live with the consequences.

The next two case studies will look at manufacturing and retail.

The biggest difference between these businesses and the ones we have already talked about is inventory and customer credit. While every industry will have unique characteristics that are important to monitor, all businesses will have many aspects that are the same.

Case study #3: Andy's Bird Houses

Andy Sanchez started building bird houses out of metal years ago—mostly for family members. It was basically just a hobby. People kept telling him the houses were unique and beautiful and he should expand and sell them on the internet. Andy and his wife had a little money but not enough to start a business and he mostly just wanted to make a little extra money and enjoy his quiet time building bird houses.

His brother, Charlie, had graduated with a degree in finance and was working for a large bank downtown. Charlie had been involved in some deals and his fees from those deals had made him wealthy, at least by Sanchez family standards. Charlie wanted to back Andy and kept pushing the idea. Charlie was convinced that the product was unique and very marketable. He thought it could make them both millionaires.

Charlie still didn't have Andy's okay, but he formed a company anyway, A. C. Birdhouses, LLC. He also started to put together a pitch book. He was telling Andy that he could raise millions. The whole thing made Andy very nervous. The thing that intrigued him, though, was being able to buy the right equipment to manufacture the bird houses to the quality standards he really wanted. He loved machines. Just to appease his brother, he developed a list of equipment he would need, and the size of space needed for a shop. From that Charlie built a schedule for capital that would be needed (Chart 31).

Andy was stunned. He had no idea his brother was thinking about something this large. His first question was how many bird

	Option 1	Option 2	Option 3
Size of Shop (sq.ft.)	12,500	15,000	17,500
Leasehold Improvement ($3/sq.ft)	$ 37,500	$ 45,000	$ 52,500
Heavy Equipment	$ 125,000	$ 175,000	$ 200,000
Break Room Equipment	$ 2,500	$ 2,500	$ 2,500
Cleaning Equipment	$ 3,500	$ 3,500	$ 3,500
Advertising	$ 32,000	$ 50,000	$ 65,000
Web Site	$ 5,500	$ 5,500	$ 5,500
Licensing / Patents	$ 4,500	$ 4,500	$ 4,500
Office Equipment	$ 2,500	$ 2,500	$ 3,500
Computers	$ 18,000	$ 22,000	$ 35,000
Miscellaneous	$ 4,500	$ 5,500	$ 6,500
Shipping Equipment	$ 3,500	$ 3,500	$ 3,500
Material Inventory	$ 12,000	$ 14,000	$ 16,000
Finished Product Inventory	$ 55,000	$ 65,000	$ 75,000
Wages Prior to Opening	$ 18,500	$ 18,500	$ 18,500
Total	$ 324,500	$ 417,000	$ 491,500
Working Capital	$ 125,000	$ 145,000	$ 165,000
Total Investment Capital	**$ 449,500**	**$ 562,000**	**$ 656,500**

Chart 31: Andy's Bird Houses—Initial Investment Analysis

houses would they have to sell to justify this kind of investment? Good question. Charlie didn't know but said he would figure it out.

This brought up all sorts of issues. Andy was selling his most popular bird house for $30. He once estimated that he was using about $12 in materials (which he was buying in small quantities from Home Depot), and it took him, by himself, about 4 hours to finish the house. Of course, on a large scale most of that would not be relevant—except maybe the sales price.

Most people thought for the metal bird house, with all the bells and whistles Andy built into them, the sales price was low. But if he was going to wholesale them, the retailer would want their profit. If he sold them wholesale at $30 some retailers might want to be able to sell them at $60; was that possible? He didn't think too many of his local customers would have paid $60 for a bird house.

This is the same problem we have had with all our analysis projects; how do you estimate the most critical number—sales?

Andy eventually determined that with an assembly line approach and producing 1,000 bird houses a month, he could get his costs down to $12.50 per bird house including materials and labor. Based on his overhead calculations, he decided a good wholesale price could be $25.00—this included simplifying the design and eliminating some of the added features he had been including but decided they were too complicated for a factory environment.

The $50 retail price still worried Andy, but maybe it would be marketable. Charlie thought it was all great—Charlie was a deal maker, and he was hyper excited. He said the 1,000 sales number was a slam dunk; Andy just shook his head.

Andy was pretty good at "figuring" things, so he decided to do a little analysis himself. He went and looked at some warehouse/factory space. He stayed on the low-end for size and was amazed how big a 12,500 square foot building was. He talked to some owners and realtors to get some ballpark numbers on rent and utilities. He was sure all of that was much higher than Charlie had guessed.

He decided to make his own guess at what a break-even sales number would be. Most of the fixed overhead cost was easy to

Break-Even Calculation		
Fixed Costs/Overhead (monthly)	$	31,250
Variable Costs/Overhead		56%
100% minus variable costs		44%
Fixed divided by (100%-variable)		$31,250÷44%
Monthly Break-even	**$**	**71,022**
Proof		
Revenue	$	71,022
Fixed Expenses	$	31,250
Variable Direct Costs	$	34,091
Variable Overhead	$	5,682
Total Expenses	$	71,022
Profit/Loss	$	-
Number of Bird Houses		
Break-Even Revenue (monthly)	$	71,022
Price per House	$	25
Number of Bird Houses per Month		2,841
Number of Bird Houses per Year		34,091

Chart 32: Andy's Bird Houses—Break-Even Analysis

determine within a range. The variable overhead was more difficult. For the product based on his estimates the direct variable costs would be 32% materials and 16% labor. Some of those costs would not be able to determine until the complete assembly line was designed. He thought his estimate was valid for his purposes.

Many of the overhead costs tied to the building were also fairly easy to get. He talked to the building people about utilities, and they shared some historical numbers based on the last tenant. All the numbers felt massive to Andy. He ended up estimating all fixed costs at \$31,250 and all variable at 56% (see Chart 32).

That was to break even. Nobody is going to invest \$500,000 to break even. Andy did not know the investment world like Charlie, but he guessed a return between 12% and 18% would be a low target with something in the 20s a high target return. What would that do to the number of birdhouses? Without a lot of pencil pushing, he guessed it would be approaching 4,000 per month. He just shook his head.

That night he talked to his wife. He told her he would do this if she wanted, but he hated the idea of running a factory with a bunch of people working for investors who only cared about a return on their investment. He told her they had a secure retirement and all he really wanted to do was build a few bird houses to make a bit extra and to make people happy. She smiled and gave a quick kiss— "you cannot be your brother. Tell him no."

Charlie was very angry when Andy told him. Charlie said the 4,000 number was nothing, he thought they could build 10,000. That only made Andy more sure he was making the right decision, enough would never be enough in Charlie's world.

Andy told Charlie he would lease them the rights to the designs with all of his sketches and he would help them get it up and running for a royalty of \$2 per house. Charlie got a smile on his face and began to negotiate—he loved to dicker. They agreed on a \$1.25 per house and Charlie left—smiling; he had won that round.

Andy went back to his comfortable garage workshop and built birdhouses. Charlie would come by every once in a while, or they would talk at family gatherings. He was always right on the verge of talking to the right investor, and he would have all the money in a few weeks.

After several years Charlie stopped bringing it up. Andy was selling between 20 and 30 birdhouses a month and was very happy.

Note: Planning, especially a new business, is often about deciding if you want to go into that business. That has been mentioned throughout this book, it is very important to understand your risks before you commit to a large financial and personal obligation. Almost everyone has had the experience of deciding you hate your work life, and you want to try something on your own—I think that is great. Just make sure you spend the time to understand what is at risk and evaluate the likelihood of success or failure. In the study above Andy made a personal decision about what he wanted his life to be, not based only on money, but based on what would make him happy. He thought about managing the birdhouse factory and knew he would hate it; he thought about dealing with investors questioning his every decision about his birdhouses and knew he would hate it. Andy went beyond numbers to forecast the future and didn't like what he saw. That is a part of planning—and maybe, the most important part.

Case study #4: "Everybody's" Next Big Thing

The next big thing is usually tied to tech, either something very new or a new take on something already done. This is the next Tik Tok, or the next Facebook, or the next Google or the next . . . *it has never been done before.*

What these deals have in common is that there is no way of knowing what will happen. Estimating the future revenue and/or profits from these types of ventures is near impossible. Many high-tech ideas can go from nothing to millions of customers in a blink of the eye. This means any sort of "reasonable" analysis probably will not impress anyone—and almost all these deals will be funded with someone else's money.

This is a game played in a different ballpark than the more common sport of small business. And my expertise here is very limited.

Even with that said, all business deals have a goal—to make money for someone. When presenting your idea for the "Next Big Thing", concentrate on the idea. Let the money guys develop their own understanding of the billions that can be made if this turns out to be . . . ?

Case study #5: Ma's Pie Delivery

Mrs. Clark's homemade pies were famous in her hometown and a big hit at every church social. Her son Chad thinks he could build a business delivering his mom's pie in the big city he had moved to some years ago to work for the government (a job he hates). His mother told him he should stick with his dependable job, because he had a great retirement and health plan. Chad was only 26 years old and could not even imagine retirement—he wanted to make a fortune in pie delivery right now.

This delivery business could be called a service business (delivery), a retail business (selling purchased pies), a manufacturing business (making Ma's pies) and a tech business (web site, app), all wrapped into one.

Chad's background did not include any of these business models.

Note: My advice to Chad would be go work for someone in the food business and learn some more before you venture off into the unknown world. I have given that advice before, it is often ignored.

Chad had decided he would buy "standard" pies from a local bakery and resell those pies delivered, plus he would lease a professional kitchen and bake his mom's recipes for resell delivered. He was going to do that without his mom or anyone else who knew how to bake a pie—the obvious flaw in his plans was being ignored at this stage.

He was going to need some space. He had decided from the beginning that he would not be selling at retail—it would only be delivery. He still needed space for refrigeration equipment to store

	Option 1 (Plan)	Option 2 (Middle)	Option 3 (Highest)
Storage Space			
Leasehold Improvements	$ 2,500	$ 5,000	$ 7,500
Equipment—Refrigeration	$ 2,500	$ 3,500	$ 4,500
Equipment—Other	$ 1,500	$ 3,500	$ 7,500
Miscellaneous	$ 1,500	$ 2,000	$ 2,500
Total—Storage Space	$ 8,000	$ 14,000	$ 22,000
Leased Equipment			
Leased Kitchen	$ 750	$ 1,250	$ 1,850
Equipment/Tools	$ 800	$ 1,200	$ 1,500
Miscellaneous	$ 500	$ 750	$ 1,000
Total—Leased Equipment	$ 2,050	$ 3,200	$ 4,350
Other			
Communication	$ 1,800	$ 3,500	$ 3,500
Computers/Internet	$ 2,000	$ 4,000	$ 6,000
Video/Audio Equipment	$ 500	$ 4,000	$ 5,000
Wages Prior to Opening	$ 3,500	$ 3,500	$ 3,500
Total—Other	$ 7,800	$ 15,000	$ 18,000
Total Investment	$ 17,850	$ 32,200	$ 44,350
Working Capital	$ 8,500	$ 12,000	$ 14,500
Total Investment Capital	**$ 26,350**	**$ 44,200**	**$ 58,850**

Chart 33: Ma's Pies—Initial Investment Analysis

the pies. The shelf life of pies was relatively short—another major complication he had not given much thought.

Where he was most comfortable (and knowledgeable) was

marketing, promotion, social media, web sites and the app. Chad had attended a Community College in his new town for a couple of semesters taking night classes on these subjects—he had not done anything in the real world with these skills.

He had no financial background, so, he asked his brother-in-law to help with the numbers—after all, he worked at an accounting firm. Unfortunately, his brother-in-law only did taxes and said he had no idea how to evaluate his business idea. The brother-in-law pawned him off on an older man who worked in the firm and was their small business specialist. None of that worked out because they offered to do the analysis for a fee that Chad found absurd. The first of many, many times Chad would bump into the problem of not having the money to do what was needed to make his business a success.

He next approached a person he had met in one of his classes at the community college. Jack had said he was studying business, so with this small clue Chad thought he might know how to evaluate the pie delivery business. Long story short, Chad eventually met Jack's sister Jill, who was a business analysist for a local bank. She said she could evaluate the business idea, but she was wanting something for her effort. They settled on Jill owning 10% of the non-existent business. Chad had not asked Jill to sign anything and was ready to charge on.

Note: Business partners or ex-business partners can become the bane of your existence if you do not handle matters properly. Never discuss business ideas without getting an NDA (non-disclosure agreement). It may not stop someone from stealing your idea, but it will slow them down and will give you some legal foundation for suing them. NDA's have gotten a bum rap due to people using them to keep others from sharing private information that is secret only because it is em-barrassing or illegal. In the business world the NDA is to protect you

	Plan
Storage Space	
Leasehold Improvements	$ 1,850
Equipment—Refrigeration	$ 2,500
Equipment—Other	$ 800
Miscellaneous	$ 750
Total—Storage Space	$ 5,900
Leased Equipment	
Leased Kitchen	$ 750
Equipment/Tools	$ 800
Miscellaneous	$ 500
Total—Leased Equipment	$ 2,050
Other	
Communication	$ 1,450
Computers/Internet	$ 1,800
Video/Audio Equipment	$ 500
Wages Prior to Opening	$ 2,200
Total—Other	$ 5,950
Total Investment	$ 13,900
Working Capital	$ 8,100
Total Investment Capital	**$ 22,000**

Chart 34: Ma's Pies—Initial Investment Analysis, Updated

from someone taking confidential business information that was disclosed in confidence and using it to your harm.

Who knows if Jill will turn out to be a good "partner", but she

	Lower	Break-Even	Better
Sales			
Pies Sold Per Day	15	27	45
Average Price of Pie	$ 22.50	$ 22.50	$ 22.50
Sales per Day	$ 338	$ 605	$ 1,013
Sales per Week	$ 2,363	$ 4,237	$ 7,088
Sales per Month	$ 9,923	$ 17,794	$ 29,768
Yearly Net Sales	**$ 119,070**	**$ 213,532**	**$ 357,210**
Revenue—Detail			
Number of Pies Resold	2,184	3,917	6,552
Number of Pies Made	3,276	5,875	9,828
Total Pies Sold	5,460	9,792	16,380
Direct Costs			
Pies—Resold	$ 13,650	$ 24,479	$ 40,950
Pies—Made	$ 19,165	$ 34,369	$ 57,494
Total Direct Food/Labour	**$ 32,815**	**$ 58,848**	**$ 98,444**
Delivery Fee (per pie)	$ 4.50	$ 4.50	$ 4.50
Delivery Costs	$ 24,570	$ 44,062	$ 73,710
Packaging	$ 6,006	$ 10,771	$ 18,018
Total Direct Other Costs	**$ 30,576**	**$ 54,833**	**$ 91,728**
Total Direct Costs	**$ 63,391**	**$ 113,680**	**$ 190,172**
Gross Margin	**$ 55,679**	**$ 99,852**	**$ 167,038**

Chart 35: Ma's Pies—Revenue and Cost Assumptions
(Continued on next page)

	Lower	Break-Even	Better
Gross Margin (from prev. pg.)	$ 55,679	$ 99,852	$ 167,038
Overhead			
Utilities	$ 4,200	$ 4,200	$ 4,200
Advertising	$ 10,000	$ 10,000	$ 10,000
Insurance	$ 3,500	$ 3,500	$ 3,500
Web/Internet	$ 4,500	$ 4,500	$ 4,500
Rent/Phones/Misc.	$ 10,400	$ 10,400	$ 10,400
Accounting/Legal	$ 3,500	$ 3,500	$ 3,500
Cleaning	$ 2,400	$ 2,400	$ 2,400
Variable OH (0.06 × Sales)	$ 7,144	$ 12,812	$ 21,433
Total Overhead	$ 45,644	$ 51,312	$ 59,933
Profit before taxes & OC	$ 10,035	$ 48,540	$ 107,106
Owner's Compensation	$ 48,500	$ 48,500	$ 48,500
Profit before taxes, after OC	$ (38,465)	$ 40	$ 58,606

Chart 35, Concluded

knew her stuff when it came to financial analysis.

Chad had saved a little, but not nearly the amounts Jill was planning. Chad did have five siblings and had talked to all of them about his idea. He told them about Jill and that he had offered her 10% to do the financial analysis and to help in financial planning once the business was opened. One sister thought that was stupid but didn't have a good option so let it go. Chad had made a proposal that he would get 30% of the business and would invest $5,000, he was wanting each of his siblings to invest $5,000 and they would each receive 12% of the business.

That would put them at a total investment of $30,000 which, based in Jill's analysis, was the lowest number they could get by with. Chad said he thought he could shave some dollars off Jill's investment list and get the total with working capital down to closer to $22,000. They all agreed and shook hands. Once again, no documents were signed.

Note: Always have legal documents prepared for any major business decisions between partners. Even family members. Often disputes arise later because someone remembers past events differently. Signed documents do not mean you don't trust your family partners; it is just good business practice.

Jill advised Chad that going with the least and reducing that any further increased the likelihood that they would run out of money. She advised that each family member should invest $7,500, including Chad, which would put them at $45,000 capital and would significantly lower the risk. Chad ignored her.

Chad began to work with Jill to build the first year forecasted income statement. There were several areas where Chad had not fully thought through everything. First was the delivery method. There were services available to offer delivery for a fee—Chad did not know the fee. Or they could employ their own drivers in a limited delivery area. Chad did not like that idea because that would put more pressure on him to hire and manage the drivers.

After doing some research and making some calls Jill decided to use a 20% estimate for third party delivery. She thought this might create some problems with the numbers but was not sure until she did the work.

Jill was starting to like what she was seeing. She did not believe you could start the business on Chad's $22,000, but on $50,000 you might have something. She had no idea if you could sell 45 pies a day or not; but if you could, you could make over a 100% return on your investment.

Her guess was that you would sell more than one pie at a time so the average customer account would be much less than the 45 pies per day, maybe as low as 20. Twenty customers per day started to sound very reasonable. The third-party delivery seemed high but she had done research and thought the average price of $22.50 was not out of line. Now the big question—do people still eat pies every day or is it only on holidays?

Once again, the biggest question on any business proposal will be how reasonable are your sales projections. Jill wasn't sure about revenue projections, but she sure liked the low investment and potential high return. She called her husband.

Well, as you might have guessed by now, Jill stole Chad's idea and opened her own pie delivery business—Grannies Pies on the Go. Nobody has seen the financial numbers yet, but currently all parties are in a nasty lawsuit with only Jill smiling (which would seem to suggest her thieving ways have paid off).

Chad never opened his business. When Jill stabbed him in the back, he decided maybe self-employment was not for him. He went back to his government job and is looking forward to his next vacation. He often tells people he was the original founder of the national chain Grannies Pies on the Go; but few believe him. He didn't take any of his sibling's money, but they are still angry at him because they missed out on Grannies Pies.

Appendix: Cash Accounting versus Accrual Accounting

Everything that has been explored in this book was based on Accrual Accounting. The simplest way to explain accrual accounting has to do with one of the basic principles of accounting, the Matching Principle.

The Matching Principle is that revenues and their costs and expenses should match in any accounting period being examined. Revenues are recognized when earned and costs/expenses are recognized when they are used to generate revenues. This can sound simple, but also can become amazingly complicated.

If we look at the transactions in Charts 36A-36C, we can see the difference between cash basis and accrual basis accounting. On a cash basis these transactions over three months generated a loss of $4,200. On an accrual basis there was a profit of $5,108.

The differences are all timing issues. The cash basis is your checkbook—it reflects money received and cash spent; regardless of how it has impacted the business. This cash balance is very important and there are reports to give you that information; but the profit or loss of the business is calculated based on a particular period for both revenue and costs/expenses and does not care when you will receive the revenue or when you will pay for the costs.

The goal of accrual accounting is to match those revenues earned with the costs/expenses it took to generate those revenues.

| | Cash Basis | | | Accrual |
| | | | | |
	Cash	Non-Cash	Profit or Loss	Profit or Loss
Initial Investment	**$ 15,000**			
First Month				
Purchased Equipment *	$ (2,250)		$ (2,250)	$ (62)
Paid Rent	$ (1,250)		$ (1,250)	$ (1,250)
Paid Deposit **	$ (2,500)		$ (2,500)	
Paid Casual Labor	$ (750)		$ (750)	$ (750)
Total	$ (6,750)		$ (6,750)	$ (2,062)
Cash Balance	**$ 8,250**			
Income	$ -		$ -	$ -
Profit or Loss			**$ (6,750)**	**$ (2,062)**

Chart 36A: Accrual vs. Cash Basis Accounting, First Month
** In the Accrual method, this capital expense is spread across the life of the asset.*
*** In the Accrual method, this is a non-expense item, since it will be returned.*

In our example the company bought some equipment for $2,250 which will be used to generate revenue for 3 years (the estimated useful life of the equipment). If all that amount is expensed at once, then it is not matching the total revenue that equipment will help to produce. Using capitalization and depreciation, we will only charge each month a portion of the cost of that equipment; in this case $62 per month in depreciation. Also, in the first month a deposit was paid for utilities. This deposit will be refunded, so it is not an expense but an asset that will be fully recovered in the future. It is a cash outlay, but it just an exchange of one asset (cash) for another (deposit).

	Cash	Non-Cash	Cash Basis Profit or Loss	Accrual Profit or Loss
Cash Balance Forward	$ 8,250			
Second Month				
Paid Rent	$ (1,250)		$ (1,250)	$ (1,250)
Paid Wages	$ (4,580)		$ (4,580)	$ (4,580)
Paid Advertising	$ (980)		$ (980)	$ (980)
Bill—Food/Supplies *		$ (8,400)		$ (800)
Total	$ (6,810)		$ (6,810)	$ (7,610)
Cash Income	$ 3,500		$ 3,500	$ 3,500
Income on Credit		$ 1,500		$ 1,500
Cash Balance	$ 4,940			
Profit or Loss			$ (3,310)	$ (2,610)

Chart 36B: Accrual vs. Cash Basis Accounting, Second Month
** In the Accrual method, the expense portion is for items used during that month.*

In the next month the business receives $8,400 in food and supplies. These items will be used over several months—the only portion that is expensed this month is what was used. That is calculated by taking an inventory. Beginning inventory plus purchases minus ending inventory will equal what was used during the month.

Cash revenue was $3,500 which was for items produced during this month so it will be recorded as revenue for the month. Also, items were purchased on credit and even though no money was received it was revenue produced during the month and recorded as sales.

| | | Cash Basis | | Accrual |
	Cash	Non-Cash	Profit or Loss	Profit or Loss
Cash Balance Forward	$ 4,940			
Third Month				
Paid food bill (prv. mo.)*	$ (8,400)		$ (8,400)	$ (2,675)
Recv'd food bill (curr.)		$(2,450)		
Paid Rent	$ (1,250)		$ (1,250)	$ (1,250)
Page Wages	$ (3,250)		$ (3,250)	$ (3,250)
Paid Insurance (6 mo.) **	$ (2,800)		$ (2,800)	$ (467)
Total	$ (15,700)			
Income—Cash	$ 10,500		$ 10,500	$ 10,500
—Collected (prv. mo.)	$ 1,000		$ 1,000	
—On Credit		$ 2,250		$ 2,250
Cash Balance	$ 740			
Profit or Loss			$ (4,200)	$ 5,108
Three-Month Total			$ (14,260)	$ 436

Chart 36C: Accrual vs. Cash Basis Accounting, Third Month
** In Accrual method, expense is based on the amount of food used this month.*
*** In Accrual method, each month is accounted for one at a time.*

As you can see with this example cash and accrual show different aspects of the business. Accrual accounting is reflecting the actual financial performance of the business matching earned revenue with the costs/expenses to produce that revenue and Cash accounting monitors cash outgo and inflow—basically your check book.

The only accounting method that really tells you if your business is making a profit or operating at a loss is accrual accounting. And for those statements to be accurate someone must estimate certain amounts and adjust what was earned and what was used to create those earning. This is usually done by accountants who will make journal entries to "accrue" expenses and income.

It is for that reason that many small businesses have inaccurate accounting records—they do not want to pay an accountant to do that work and they do not know how to do it themselves. Unless you know accounting, you will have to have some help to make your records accurate. Doing financial analysis on data that is not accurate is a waste of time.

Below is more information about Cash vs. Accrual, which is from "How to Start and Run a Successful Business":

Here we go again with accounting gobbledygook. Who cares about accounting anyway? You should. What is accounting? It is a system that has certain standard rules that give you, the owner, the best tool you will have to manage your business. Many hands-on owners do not believe that statement. I'm there every day and I know what is going on, okay, maybe. The real bugaboo about accounting is that your accounting system is a mess and the information you're getting from it is garbage.

Those reports based on your very flawed accounting system is useless and should be ignored. So, is that a good reason to reject all accounting data as useless? That would be silly. If you are going to have bad accounting systems and let it stay that way, then accounting will not help you run your business. Now maybe, you would say, good, I hate accounting. That is bad business. Do big companies spend a ton of money on accounting, you better believe it. Is that because the CEO of Big Biz, Inc. is an accountant and he just loves numbers, hell, no. It's because that is the only way a CEO can tell what is going on with his vast enterprise.

A small business owner can say I can see all my operations right here and I know what is happening. That statement can be true, but in most cases, it is just a myth the owner has developed that he knows what is happening. He can see the theft of critical supplies that occurs at night, he can't see the flawed invoicing that is not properly billing the customers. The best way for the owner to have a handle on his business is through numbers—his accounting system.

There is some discussion of accounting systems in the appendix, but this book's scope can't begin to cover the right accounting software for your firm or how to make it work for you. I will say I have used QuickBooks for small business and for medium sized business and it works. Do others work, sure. It's accounting and the rules are the same. The most critical part of the accounting system is the business owner, if the owner thinks it's a waste of time to emphasize the need for good accounting, then his employees will ignore all the accounting requirements to secure good data, and everything will be garbage. If the owner says this is the most critical source for information about the health of my business and you will follow all rules put in place to get good numbers, then it will happen. I would like to preach some more about the importance of a good accounting system and the employees or outside skill people to make it work, but I will move on now—but let me say once more, this is as critical as anything you do as a business owner to ensure your success—invest in a good accounting system and the people to make it work.

One aspect of accounting that I think most small business owners do not completely understand is the difference between cash and accrual accounting. Conceptually, a business owner can understand cash accounting. You count revenue as cash received and you deduct expenses when they are paid. Easy. I took in $500 today and paid out $300, I made $200. Easy, I must be a CPA!

Now you have a truck payment you make at the first of the month, you have insurance you pay quarterly, you have some maintenance cost you pay when something breaks, you have a new AC unit you just put in the office which you paid in full, you have rent you pay once a month—along with other expenses occurring irregularly. So did you really make $200, of course not. Common sense says all those other costs need to be distributed to figure out profit or loss.

Accrual accounting attempts to meet one of the basic accounting standards, the matching of revenue with expenses for any period. If you had an annual insurance payment you made in January, accrual accounting would expense one twelfth of that expense each month. Or if you buy a truck, it would not be fully expensed the day you bought it but set up as an asset and the expense distributed each month based on the life of the truck. So, a truck with a cost of $25,000 and a salvage value of $5,000 and a useful life of years would be allocated each month at $416.66, expensing the entire net cost of $20,000 distributed over 48 months. An even better method would be to distribute the cost based on the actual use as measure by mileage.

The point of accrual accounting is the match the revenue earned with the cost associated with earning that revenue. The purpose is to give a more exact picture of what the business has "really" earned, not what cash was collected minus what was disbursed.

The only accounting system that has value to a business owner is the accrual accounting system. Cash basis may supply a method to do taxes which might be in the owner's benefit, but cash-based accounting does not give you any exact operational information you can use to manage the business.

Another area of accounting that is less likely to come into play in a small business but is just as important, is cost accounting. Cost accounting will be the systems used on manufacturing (which can include food service). This set of rules is trying to capture all elements that go into a product. If you were a small furniture manufacture, you would want to use cost accounting to make sure you're pricing your product to generate a profit. You know the cost of wood, but how about overhead, how much of that should be included in each table?

I know I am repeating myself, but accounting is just a tool. If you take the time (and spend the money) to understand this tool, it will help you be a better businessperson and will increase your chances of being successful.

Stay in Touch

Stay in touch with Ted Clifton and Success Paths business books. Clifton's background is financial (CPA, Controller, CFO) with over 30 years of real-world experience as a financial advisor, business owner of fifteen business ventures and as a business broker with valuation experience.

Learn more about successful business practices and small business matters, such as selling or buying a business, starting and running a small business and how to value a small business.

Newsletters are free and informative. Opt-out at any time. Thanks for your interest in Success Paths Business Books.

Subscribe today at:
https://mailchi.mp/1e966d569a72/success-paths

Ted Clifton Mystery Books

Business books and mystery books might be an odd combination, but maybe they are connected in a mysterious way—if you enjoy mysteries, check out these offerings from Ted Clifton. Learn more at **www.tedclifton.com**.

Pacheco & Chino Mysteries—A retired sheriff, an enigmatic bait-shop owner, and an Apache fishing guide team up to solve a mystery that starts with an out-of-place show dog—and ends much deadlier.

The Bootlegger's Legacy—Joe and Mike, middle-aged losers, have uncovered a promise of abundant riches—if only they can solve the clues left behind by Mike's bootlegger dad.

Vincent Malone—Disgraced investigator and alcoholic Vincent Malone finds new life as a shuttle driver for a B&B—then a guest is murdered and his investigative skills are suddenly front-and-centre again.

The Muckraker Series—New journalism grad Tommy Jacks hires on as a political reporter with a struggling paper, but is quickly pulled into an ugly newspaper war when a rival reporter is murdered.

continued on next page…

Ted Clifton Series Starter Set—Amazon ebook containing the complete first books of the Pacheco & Chino, Vincent Malone, and Muckraker mystery series.

Have questions or comments for Ted Clifton? He can be reached at ask@tedclifton.com.

Thanks for being a reader!